VEGAN CAKES

AND OTHER BAKES

Jérôme Eckmeier
Daniela Lais

VEGAN CAKES

AND OTHER BAKES

80 easy vegan recipes

cookies, cakes, pizzas, breads, and more

CONTENTS

VEGAN BASICS

PREFACE

Our aim for this book was for the recipes to be quick and simple to make, and, ideally, to avoid exotic ingredients. The German Vegetarian Association asked, "What vegan baking recipes would you like?" and over 600 of our Facebook friends responded. They loved wholesome foods, cookies, and muffins – and they dreamt of the perfect vegan "cheesecake".

Their careful, detailed responses show that baking is a hot topic for people who want to follow a vegan diet – whether for some or all of the time – because purely plant-based cakes, biscuits, breads, and rolls are hard to find. Furthermore, information provided at bakeries isn't always reliable; for example, often you can't be sure if the margarine they use really is vegan.

So, for our second book with Vegetarian Society's kitchen buddy Jérôme Eckmeier, there was never any doubt that our topic would have to be baking. Jérôme was supported on this project by our new discovery, baking expert Daniela Lais. Together they met the vegan's requests: that the recipes should be easy for anyone to follow, with clear, step-by-step instructions, for example on how to make muffins super fluffy and "cheesecake" silky smooth.

So even if you rarely venture into a kitchen: it's time to get baking! Find out what fun baking can be, how it saves money, and how it makes your home smell heavenly, too. These sweet temptations are fantastic ambassadors for veganism.

It's true that anyone who wants to bake great cakes needs a few key ingredients... but eggs, butter, lard, and milk most definitely aren't necessary.

Yours,
Sebastian Zösch
Managing director of the German Vegetarian Association
[Vegetarierbund Deutschland e.V.]

PS
Find us at
www.vebu.de and
facebook.com/ provegDE

THE VEGGIE COMMUNITY TOP TEN

What is your favourite baked item: the thing you can't bear to be without, even as a vegan? A survey by the German Vegetarian Association helped identify which baking recipes the veggie community would most like while avoiding milk, eggs, and so on. The results were used as inspiration for the recipes in this book.

1. CHEESECAKE PP. 80–85

2. COOKIES PP. 38–39

3. CUPCAKES / MUFFINS PP. 28–33

4. CHRISTMAS COOKIES PP. 170–185

5. MARBLED CHOCOLATE CHEESECAKE PP. 54–55

6. SPONGE PP. 86–87; 187

7. MARBLE CAKE (ZEBRA CAKE) PP. 50–51

8. BLACK FOREST GATEAU PP. 106–107

9. BROWNIES PP. 34–37

10. WAFFLES PP. 24–25

BASIC EQUIPMENT

With tried and tested recipes, a few techniques, tricks, and skills, plus the right utensils, vegan baking is just as simple as conventional baking, and sometimes even simpler.

MUST HAVES

Measuring jug, saucepans, frying pans, fine sieve, large and small spoons, paring knife or potato peeler, graters, pastry brush, chopping board, rolling pin, kitchen scales (ideally digital), toothpicks or skewer for testing. Also:

Mixing bowls

For preparing most recipes, two mixing bowls are enough. Often dry ingredients are combined in one bowl and liquid ingredients in a second bowl. For beating cream, we also recommend a mixing bowl with a lid with an opening for the beaters.

Baking tins

High-quality baking tins made of metal or silicone are crucial for the success of many baked items. We recommend a springform tin and, where required, a pie dish, a loaf tin, a 12-hole muffin tin or silicone tray, and a rectangular ovenproof (glass) dish, for bakes like brownies. If your baking tin isn't quite the right size, just adjust the quantities and baking times.

Baking paper

Environmentally friendly, washable baking paper, which can be reused again and again, or some simple coated baking paper. Different sizes are helpful.

Electric hand whisk

For preparing cream, frostings, or toppings, at least 450 watt.

NICE TO HAVE

The decision to purchase additional kitchen gadgets is entirely down to the individual, but the items here are often highly practical, save time, and can help to make baked goods look even more attractive.

Cake ring

This holds cakes in shape during filling or stacking and helps ensure accurate alignment where there are multiple layers to a cake.

Dough scraper, spatula, and palette knife

These help smooth out the surface on creamy layers and other spreadable substances and can be used to straighten up edges.

Piping bag with nozzles

Piping bags made from reusable material are easy to use and to clean. Recommended nozzles are:
• a 14–16mm star nozzle
• a variety of 18mm nozzles for decorating cupcakes
• a flower nozzle
• a round nozzle.
Adapters make it easy to change nozzles quickly by screwing and unscrewing, but you can also make a simple piping bag yourself (see p.188).

Zester or box grater

This makes it easy to remove and zest the peel on citrus fruit and shreds the zest evenly, making it ideal for decorative purposes.

Waffle iron

Use this for sweet and savoury waffles – ideally a classic heart-shaped iron. Oiling the surface makes cleaning easier.

Food processor for grinding or mixing

This is an optional luxury for preparing cakes that are made with raw ingredients or which do not involve baking. It grinds and mixes thoroughly in a single process.

STORE CUPBOARD ESSENTIALS

One advantage of vegan baking is that most of the ingredients keep for longer than animal products, which can go off very easily. It is super easy to rustle up a delicious cake with a very modest supply of high-quality, organic ingredients, which you can keep stocked in your store cupboard.

Plain flour
Shelf life: if stored in an airtight container, away from the light and in a dry location at 16–20°C (60.8–68°F), up to 1 year

Fine cane sugar
Shelf life: if stored in an airtight container, away from the light and in a dry location at 16–20°C (60.8–68°F), up to 1 year or longer

Baking powder
Shelf life: if stored in an airtight container in a dry location and unopened, 1½ years or longer

Dry yeast
Shelf life: if stored in an airtight container in a dry location and unopened, up to 2 years

Soya milk
Shelf life: kept sealed, even if not chilled, several months

Flavourless oil, for example, rapeseed oil
Shelf life: kept sealed and airtight in a cool dark location, at least 1 year

Vanilla extract
Shelf life: kept sealed in a cool, dark place, 6 months to 1 year. Pure vanilla extract has an indefinite shelf life

Vegan margarine
Shelf life: 6–8 weeks

"LIGHTNING" CAKES

For a 25cm (10in) long loaf tin

400g (14oz)	plain wheat flour, plus some extra for the tin
180g (6¼oz)	fine cane sugar
1	sachet baking powder
250ml (9fl oz)	soya milk
120ml (4fl oz)	rapeseed oil
1–2 tsp	vanilla extract
	margarine, for greasing the tin

Preparation: 5 minutes + 1 hour baking time

Preheat the oven to 180°C (350°F/Gas 4). Stir the dry ingredients together in a bowl. Whisk the soya milk, rapeseed oil, and vanilla extract and add to bowl, mixing everything until smooth. Transfer the mixture to a loaf tin, greased and dusted with flour, and bake for about 1 hour, until an inserted wooden skewer comes out clean.

TIP:

Substitute 100g (3½oz) of flour with the same quantity of ground hazelnuts, ground almonds, or coconut flakes. If desired, you can also add spices, finely chopped vegan chocolate chunks or dried fruits from your store-cupboard supplies.

KNOW HOW – TECHNIQUES, TIPS, AND TRICKS

In order to avoid eggs, milk, and cream, vegan baking has to use other ingredients to strengthen and stabilize bakes and to create light, moist, and tasty dishes. With the right ingredients and techniques, this is not a problem.

Vinegar as a catalyst
Cider vinegar is best for vegan baking. You won't be able to taste the vinegar at all in the finished cake, but it helps the baking soda unleash its power and, when combined with soya milk, it improves the quality of the baked product. Whisk soya milk and vinegar together in a bowl; the acetic acid thickens the soya milk after about 5 minutes. Stir the mixture into your other ingredients to make light cakes and pastries with a fine texture.

Mixing with a spoon
With many vegan recipes, it is important not to "over stir" the mixture, so ingredients should be mixed gently with a spoon. The carbon dioxide in mineral water can potentially make the mixture lighter and fluffier, and the addition of leavening agents, such as yeast and bicarbonate of soda, also help the dough rise and lighten beautifully. Mixing with an electric whisk or stirring for too long or too vigorously would destroy the resulting air bubbles, making the dough too heavy and stopping it from rising properly. Mixtures should not be left to stand for too long after stirring; instead they should be baked promptly, as soon as the leavening agents have been allowed to work fully, so that the mixture rises well. Any fillings, such as fruit, should be washed and chopped before preparing the mixture so they can be added quickly.

Sweeten properly
Always use fine cane sugar. Coarse cane sugar is best avoided as it doesn't dissolve easily, particularly in shortcrust pastry. Coarse sugar can impede or even completely prevent the mix from rising. In dark mixtures prepared with lots of cocoa powder, coarse cane sugar crystals can remain visible – indicating that the sugar has failed to dissolve. This means the sugar won't evenly sweeten the baked item.

Gelling and setting
Agar-agar is a good plant-based gelling agent, most commonly available in powdered form. Since it has powerful bonding capabilities, it is used very sparingly: ½ tsp agar-agar is enough for about 250ml (9fl oz) liquid. The fine powder is stirred into cold liquid, which is briefly brought to the boil, simmered for a few minutes, then quickly stirred into the mixture that needs to set. The liquid will only set once it has cooled down completely. Alcohol reduces the setting properties, as do citrus fruits and their juices, due to their acidity.

Whipping cream
Always make sure your soya, rice, or coconut whipping cream is well chilled and beat it at top speed using an electric hand mixer for at least 3 minutes, until the cream is nice and stiff. Rice cream is less firm in consistency after whisking than soya or coconut cream so, if using this, we recommend you sprinkle in some cream stiffener about half way through whisking, before continuing to beat. If the cream is chilled again after beating, it will set even more firmly and is particularly good for piped decorations.

Oven temperatures
Unless otherwise specified, the temperatures provided in this book refer to non-fan settings. For fan ovens, the temperature should be lowered by about 20°C (68°F).

SIMPLY VEGANISED

Nowadays most animal products can easily be replaced with plant-based equivalents, sometimes by simply combining two or three ingredients with each other.

Butter	Vegan margarine
Buttermilk	1 part soya milk + 1 part soya yogurt + 1 splash lemon juice
Cream	Soya cream, rice cream, coconut cream, or oat cream
Cream cheese	Mix 500g (1lb 2oz) soya yogurt with 400g (14oz) cashews at maximum power until you have a fine, creamy purée. Decant into a bowl, cover securely with cling film, and leave to ferment at room temperature for 24 hours.
Gelatine	Agar-agar
Honey	Agave syrup, maple syrup
Milk	Soya milk, oat milk, almond milk, spelt milk, rice milk, hemp milk, or other nut milks
Quark	Soya quark, silken tofu. Alternatively, line a sieve with a clean linen cloth and place it over a bowl. Add unsweetened soya yogurt, and twist the ends of the cloth together firmly at the top, fixing them in place with a rubber band. Place in the fridge overnight and squeeze out any excess liquid.
Sour cream	1 part soya yogurt + 1 part soya cream + 1 splash lemon juice, or alternatively, finely puréed silken tofu
Whipped egg whites	Ener-g Egg Replacer
Yogurt	Soya yogurt

INSTEAD OF 1 EGG

There are various options for replacing eggs, but the ingredients should always be chosen to suit the flavour of the relevant recipe.

1 tsp egg substitute powder + 3½ tbsp water (follow instructions on pack)

60g (2oz) apple purée

1 tbsp chickpea flour mixed with 2 tbsp water

½ a large, very ripe banana, finely mashed

1 tbsp ground linseed mixed with 3 tbsp water, leave to stand for 10 minutes – only use for dark mixtures because the brown dots will be visible in pale mixtures

1 tbsp soya flour mixed with 2 tbsp water – rule of thumb: replaces up to 3 eggs

11

BRIEF PRODUCT INFORMATION

Agar-agar is a plant-based alternative to gelatine made from algae and mainly available in powder form. Agar-agar is absolutely tasteless.

Agave syrup is a sweetener that is free from commercial industrial sugar and can be used as a 1:1 substitute for honey. Agave syrup has a slightly less intense flavour than maple syrup.

Bicarbonate of soda (sodium hydrogen carbonate) is a leavening agent that is an ingredient in baking powder (which also contains an additional acidifier). Bicarbonate of soda only takes effect when it is combined with acidic ingredients, such as vinegar or lemon, and it helps to make cakes light and fluffy.

Cheese is often used in savoury baking recipes. Vegan cheese varieties with good melting properties include MozzaRisella, Nutcrafter Creamery, and No-Moo Melty from Vegusto.

Egg substitute products are powders you can buy made from starch and thickening agents.

Fine cane sugar has the best baking properties; it has a subtle caramel flavour and is pleasantly sweet. It is produced by squeezing out the sugar cane and boiling the juice to make a syrup to which tiny sugar crystals are added. These are then cleaned and dried. Alternatively, coconut sugar, birch sugar, or stevia can be used. The important thing to remember is: don't just substitute sugar 1:1 with agave syrup or maple syrup. The mixture would end up having quite different properties if you did this.

Flour is plain in most recipes. Wholemeal plain flours have more vitamins, fibre, and minerals than more refined white flours. However, you shouldn't simply use wholemeal flour as a substitute for white flour because wholemeal flour generally requires about 10 per cent more liquid. Some people cannot tolerate the gluten that is present in spelt, einkorn, emmer, green spelt, barley, oats, kamut, rye, triticale, or wheat. Gluten-free flour mixtures are available in well-stocked supermarkets and stores.

Guar gum is used in vegan baking and cooking as an egg substitute, a gelling agent, and a plant-based thickening agent. It is obtained from the seeds of the guar bean.

Linseeds are the mature seeds from the flax plant (also known as flaxseed) and should always be freshly ground as they easily go rancid if stored for long periods. Linseed is very high in fat, so it shouldn't be ground in a flour mill. It is also available for sale ready ground.

Maple syrup is another sweetener that is a good substitute for honey. Maple syrup is primarily used in American recipes, for example, for brownies or pancakes.

Margarine that is suitable for vegans is produced using palm oil, coconut oil, sunflower oil, or soya. Most vegan varieties of margarine have excellent baking properties, but some have a very high water content and should not be used for baking. A good margarine should have an original buttery taste and a nice consistency. Here, again, it's important to pay attention to the information on the package.

Oils, particularly organic oils, often have a very intense flavour. For baking you should use high-quality, flavourless baking oils so that the taste of the oil doesn't overpower the other flavours in the cake. Ideal choices for baking include rapeseed oil, sunflower oil, and corn oil.

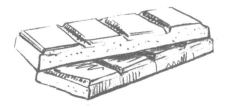

Psyllium husks are the husks of the small, dark, shiny seeds of the Indian psyllium plantain. The husks contain high levels of swelling agents and mucilage, so they are used as a plant-based swelling agent.

Silken tofu has a soft, gel-like consistency and is ideal for combining with other ingredients for baking.

Soya and soya products should be purchased carefully. Select organic soya products made from European soya beans. These are guaranteed to be GMO-free and haven't been transported over huge distances.

Soya cream/soya cream substitutes, like rice or oat creams, are not generally suitable for whipping, but used for spreading or making a ganache. Cream substitutes specifically for whipping are also available made from soya, rice, or coconut. After whipping, rice cream has a slightly less firm consistency than soya or coconut cream, so we recommend the addition of some cream stiffener here. In contrast to the animal products, plant-based creams cannot be "over beaten".

Soya flour is a dried product obtained from the soya bean and cannot simply be replaced by other flours as none have the binding capacity of soya flour. Choose soya flour that is labelled "full fat" and never store it beyond the specified use-by date because it can easily go rancid.

Soya milk, nowadays, come in numerous varieties; some unsweetened, others sweetened or with vanilla or chocolate flavouring, and many more besides. You can use any of these, but it is important to avoid the baked product ending up too sweet or with overly dominant flavours. Savoury baked items are always prepared with unsweetened soya milk. Often for successful vegan baking it is essential to thicken the soya milk using vinegar; on no account substitute other milks for the soya milk in this case. If you are just starting out on a vegan diet, it is best to chill soya milk well before drinking and select a slightly sweetened version to get used to the rather different milk flavour.

Soya yogurt is best unsweetened for baking. If you are using already-sweetened soya yogurt or a variety with added vanilla flavouring, you will need to be careful that your mix doesn't end up too sweet and that the vanilla flavour is not too dominant.

Starch is used in some recipes for binding. Unless specified otherwise, cornflour (corn starch) is intended.

Vanilla can be bought in different forms. You can buy vanilla pods, which are slit open lengthways and the seeds scraped out using a knife. Vanilla pods are very expensive so the seeds should be used sparingly. The pods can also be ground and finely pulverised then added to your baking ingredients. Ground vanilla can be bought as a ready-made product, and vanilla pods can be stored in a jar of sugar to create "vanilla" sugar. You can also buy vanilla flavouring – vanilla essence – in liquid form.

WHAT'S WHAT – PASTRY, DOUGH, ICING, AND TOPPINGS QUICKLY EXPLAINED

Batter: The ingredients in these mixtures are simply stirred together. If desired, you can then fold in fruit or berries, or some vegetables for savoury cakes.

Biscuit dough: Biscuit dough is usually made with lots of eggs. In vegan baking, it is made without eggs, but still manages to be fluffy and moist. Pale biscuits usually contain mineral water plus vanilla as a flavouring; darker biscuits contain soya milk and cocoa powder for colouring. Baking powder and bicarbonate of soda work in conjunction with acids (for example, from a lemon) to act as leavening, or raising, agents.

Chocolate ganache: A chocolate ganache is made from a combination of chocolate and cream. Dark chocolate is finely chopped, melted, and stirred into a plant-based cream until smooth. The ganache is then spread over the cake or tart. A tip here: tilt the tray or baking tin so that the ganache can run evenly over the surface, this avoids leaving visible spoon marks when you are finished. Moist substances, such as a cream layer, should be thoroughly chilled before spreading the ganache and the chocolate ganache itself should not be too hot when it is applied.

Cupcakes: In contrast to muffins, these usually have a sugary sweet, creamy topping. They can be decorated creatively and are a great dish to bring along to an event.

Filo pastry: Filo pastry consists mainly of finely sieved flour, water, and fat. Ideally the filo pastry should be extremely thin so that you can almost see through it. The art is in working with the pastry without ripping it. You can also buy ready-made filo pastry, which is often vegan.

Frosting: Margarine, icing sugar, and a liquid are the main components in the frosting found on cupcakes or larger cakes. It is crucial that the individual ingredients are all the same temperature when being prepared. The margarine is beaten until fluffy, then icing sugar is sieved and beaten into the mix, and finally a liquid (such as syrup, or even a jam or fruit purée) is gradually added and carefully folded in.

Icing: For icing or a glaze, sieved icing sugar is stirred into a liquid. This works best with lemon juice. In order to produce a viscous, opaque, beautifully white icing, the lemon juice should only be added to the icing sugar one spoon or drop at a time and stirred until smooth. If the icing is going to be scattered with nuts or other decorations, this needs to be done relatively soon after the icing has been spread because it dries quickly.

Puff pastry: Puff pastry is a laminated dough consisting of multiple layers which puff up on baking (hence the name). The main ingredients are flour, salt, and water, then butter (or margarine for vegan baking) is incorporated in several stages. Ready-made puff pastry from the supermarket is usually vegan and is excellent for baking strudel dishes.

Shortcrust pastry: Shortcrust is often used when making biscuits, cheesecakes, or pies that have a filling. It can be pale or dark and is usually made from flour, sugar, baking powder, margarine, and possibly some water.

Yeast doughs: Consisting of flour, some salt and sugar, water or soya milk, yeast, and sometimes some oil or margarine. Temperature plays an important role when preparing yeast doughs: the temperature of the liquid that the yeast is dissolved in should be around 32°C (90°F) to enable the yeast to dissolve and let the dough rise properly. Working with dried yeast is slightly easier, as this can be stirred straight into the flour mixture.

WHERE TO FIND IT

Nowadays you can find vegan product ranges in every well-stocked supermarket, not to mention your local organic shop or health food store. Other options include vegan (mail-order) retailers, and often also Asian and Turkish food stores. Occasionally, even products which are labelled as "vegan" do in fact contain non-vegan ingredients, but this can generally be discovered from the packaging details. Read carefully and, if in doubt, ask the manufacturer!

EASY SHOPPING – VEGAN STYLE

	Supermarket	Organic shop	Health food shop	Vegan (mail-order) retailers
Agar-agar		x	x	x
Agar nectar	x	x	x	
Maple syrup	x	x	x	x
Cider vinegar	x	x	x	
Puff pastry/filo pastry	x	x		x
Egg substitute powder		x	x	x
Vegetarian cream cheese		x	x	x
Vegetarian cocoa powder	x	x	x	x
Vegetarian cheese		x	x	x
Vegetarian margarine	x	x		x
Vegetarian milk (soya, oat, almond, rice)	x	x	x	x
Vegetarian quark				x
Vegetarian cream (soya, rice, oat)	x	x	x	x
Vegetarian cream, for whipping		x	x	x
Vegetarian sour cream		x		x
Vegetarian chocolate	x	x	x	x
Silken tofu		x	x	x
Soya yogurt	x (refrigerated section)			x (and other plant-based yogurts)
Soya/chickpea flour	x (chickpea flour)	x	x	x
Vanilla, powder	x	x	x	

SWEET BITES

For breakfast, dessert, or a treat: a delicious start to the day, ideal for cookie monsters or those with a sweet tooth, and great to take along to a party.

This healthy bar gives you an instant energy boost thanks to the nutritious goji berries, high-protein moringa powder, and sweet dried fruit.

POWER BAR
WITH MORINGA

For a 20 × 20cm (8 x 8in) tin (12–16 bars)

175g (6oz)	whole almonds
90g (3¼oz)	dried apricots
100g (3½oz)	dates (ideally Medjool)
2 tbsp	agave syrup
½	seeds scraped from vanilla pod
50g (1¾oz)	goji berries
1 tbsp	moringa powder (from a health food or vegan shop)
¼ tsp	sea salt

Time: 15 mins prep + 1 day soaking

1 Soak the almonds in cold water the previous day, and soak the apricots about 30 minutes before starting preparation, then drain. Purée the almonds, apricots, dates, agave syrup, and vanilla seeds in a food processor to create a paste. Scrape the paste from the sides of the container between blitzes with a spatula.

2 Transfer the paste to a bowl, stir in the goji berries, moringa powder, and sea salt, and combine everything to make a cohesive mixture. Transfer the mixture to a tin lined with baking paper and press the mixture flat. Leave to chill thoroughly, then cut into bars.

TIP:

The power bars will keep for about 2 weeks if stored in an airtight container in the fridge, so they are ideal for preparing in larger quantities so that you can stock up on supplies.

These soft, round rolls are a delicacy that taste best if eaten fresh from the oven, either plain or with some vegan margarine and jam.

BRIOCHE ROLLS

Makes 10 rolls (or 1 x 25cm/10in loaf tin)

Time: 10 mins prep + approx. 5 hrs proving + 30 mins baking

250g (9oz)	plain flour, plus extra for dusting
1 tsp	dried yeast
50g (1¾oz)	fine cane sugar
1	pinch of salt
½	seeds scraped from vanilla pod
30g (1oz)	vegan margarine, plus extra for greasing the tin
3½ tbsp	soya milk, for brushing
40g (1¼oz)	icing sugar, for dusting

1 In a large bowl, mix together the flour, dried yeast, cane sugar, and salt. Fold in the vanilla seeds. Add 120ml (4fl oz) water and knead for about 5 minutes. Then add the margarine and knead again – it will take a while for the dough to absorb the fat. Cover and leave the dough to prove in a warm place for 45 minutes, until it has doubled in size.

2 To knock out the air from the dough, use your hands to gently work the dough into a ball. Leave it covered in the fridge for at least 3 hours, or ideally overnight. Then create 10 equal-sized rolls from the dough and place them on a baking tray lined with baking paper. Alternatively, grease a loaf tin and dust it with flour. Place the dough in the tin and smooth it out. Cover the rolls or the bread with a clean, damp tea towel and leave to rise for 1 hour until the dough has doubled in volume.

3 Preheat the oven to 180°C (350°F/Gas 4). Brush the rolls or bread with soya milk. Bake the rolls for 15–20 minutes, or the bread for 25–30 minutes, in the centre of the oven until golden. Leave to cool slightly and dust with icing sugar.

Delicious and fluffy, these pancakes are a guaranteed breakfast highlight. They are traditionally eaten with maple syrup or fresh fruit.

AMERICAN PANCAKES

Makes 4 pancakes

Time: 15 mins prep + cooking time

For the batter:

140g (5oz)	plain flour
1 tsp	bicarbonate of soda
1	pinch of salt
110ml (3¾fl oz)	soya milk or almond milk
115g (4oz)	soya yogurt
1 tbsp	rapeseed oil

Also:

flavourless oil, for cooking

maple syrup, fresh fruit, vegan chocolate drops, or jam, to serve

1 In a bowl, combine the flour with the bicarbonate of soda and salt. In a separate bowl, mix together the soya or almond milk, soya yogurt, 2 tablespoons of water, and the rapeseed oil.

2 Use a spoon to swiftly fold the liquid ingredients into the dry mixture until you have a smooth, stiff batter. Heat some oil in a pan, put dollops of about 3 tablespoons of the batter into the oil, and gently smooth them down into pancakes (don't press them completely flat, they are supposed to be slightly thick). Cook the pancakes over a moderate heat, adding some more oil if necessary. Once the pancakes are pale brown on one side, flip them over and cook on the other side.

3 Serve the pancakes straight away, with plenty of maple syrup and fresh fruit, chocolate drops, or jam, as you prefer.

TIP:

The pancakes can be served as a perfect hearty weekend breakfast, layered up with baked beans and some tofu sausages on the side. For a sweet option, try the American style of drenching the pancakes in maple syrup and garnishing with banana.

These vegan soya-free waffles can be served with a fruit coulis, jam, or simply icing sugar for a breakfast treat or for afternoon coffee with friends.

FLUFFY WAFFLES

Makes 6–8 waffles

Time: 15 mins prep + cooking time

For the batter:

390g (13½oz)	plain flour
40g (1¼oz)	fine cane sugar
2 tbsp	baking powder
½ tsp	salt
750ml (1¼ pints)	rice milk
90ml (3fl oz)	orange juice, freshly squeezed
1–2 tsp	vanilla extract
90ml (3fl oz)	rapeseed oil
1	generous splash of rum

Also:

vegan oil spray (or vegan margarine), for greasing the iron

jams, fresh fruit, icing sugar or whipped soya cream (as desired), to serve

1 To make the batter, combine the flour, cane sugar, baking powder, and salt in a bowl. In a separate bowl, whisk the rice milk with the orange juice and vanilla extract and leave to thicken for 5 minutes, then add the rapeseed oil and rum and stir all of the ingredients together until smooth.

2 Combine the liquid and dry ingredients to create a smooth batter. The batter shouldn't be left to stand for too long, so use it quickly.

3 Preheat the waffle iron and squirt it generously with an oil spray. Add a ladle of batter to the iron and cook . Repeat to make one waffle after another. Carefully remove the waffles from the iron and serve immediately with jam, fresh fruit, icing sugar, and/or soya cream.

TIP:

These fabulously fluffy waffles, made without any soya flour or egg substitute, are even more flavoursome with the addition of vanilla powder to the batter. If serving to children, leave out the rum.

PUDDING PRETZELS

Makes 8–10 pretzels

Time: 40 mins prep + 65 mins proving + 20 mins baking

For the dough:

350g (12oz)	plain flour
20g (¾oz)	fine cane sugar
1	pinch of salt
2 tsp	dried yeast
30g (1oz)	vegan margarine
200ml (7fl oz)	soya milk
270g (9½oz)	puff pastry (ready-made, see pp.14–15)

For the filling:

500ml (16fl oz)	soya milk with vanilla flavouring
60g (2oz)	instant custard powder
½	seeds scraped from vanilla pod
85g (3oz)	fine cane sugar
1	pinch of salt
20g (¾oz)	vegan margarine

For the icing:

125g (4½oz)	icing sugar
	squeeze of lemon juice

1 To make the dough, mix the flour, cane sugar, salt, and yeast in a bowl. Melt the margarine and add to the dry ingredients along with the soya milk. Knead everything to form a smooth dough, cover, and leave to prove in a warm place for about 45 minutes, until it has doubled in size.

2 Roll out the yeast dough to the same size as the puff pastry sheet (approx. 42 × 24cm/16 x 9½in). Place the dough sheet on top of the puff pastry sheet and prick all over with a fork. Fold the sheet over once and roll it out again. Then, cut into 2cm (¾in) wide strips. Twist each strip as tightly as possible and form a pretzel shape from it. Place the pretzels on a baking tray lined with baking paper, cover, and leave to prove in a warm place for 20 minutes. Preheat the oven to 180°C (350°F/Gas 4) and bake the pretzels on the middle shelf for 20 minutes. Remove from the oven and leave to cool completely.

3 For the filling, mix 200ml (7fl oz) of the soya milk with the custard powder until smooth. Place the remaining soya milk in a pan and bring to the boil over a moderate heat, adding the vanilla seeds, cane sugar, and salt. Remove the pan from the heat and add the custard powder mix, then bring to the boil again, stirring constantly. Take the pan off the heat once more, add the margarine, and stir until smooth. Leave it to cool.

4 To make the icing, sieve the icing sugar into a bowl then stir in a bit of water and lemon juice until you have a smooth, thick mixture. Coat the pretzels with the icing. Put the custard filling into a piping bag with a large star nozzle attached and pipe it into all the hollow spaces of the pretzels.

These cupcakes are great to take to a garden party, or just enjoy as a stunning and delicious treat.

BLUEBERRY CUPCAKES
WITH FRUITY FROSTING

Makes 12 cupcakes

Time: 35 mins prep + 25 mins baking

For the cupcakes:

250g (9oz)	spelt flour
¾ tsp	baking powder
¾ tsp	bicarbonate of soda
½ tsp	salt
110ml (3¾fl oz)	soya milk
1	juice and zest of small organic lemon
130ml (4½fl oz)	agave syrup
2	large, very ripe bananas
250g (9oz)	blueberries (frozen or fresh), plus
100g (3½oz)	blueberries, for decoration

For the frosting:

150g (5½oz)	soft vegan margarine
450g (1lb)	icing sugar
3–4 tbsp	blueberry syrup

1 To make the cupcakes, mix the flour with the baking powder, bicarbonate of soda, and salt in a bowl. In a separate bowl, stir together the soya milk and the lemon juice and zest and leave to thicken for about 5 minutes. Stir in the agave syrup. Peel the bananas and mash well using a fork. Add the bananas to the soya milk and agave syrup mixture and stir everything well. Stir the liquid ingredients into the dry ingredients. Finally, carefully fold in the blueberries.

2 Preheat the oven to 180°C (350°F/Gas 4). Put paper cases into the moulds in a muffin tray and divide the mixture between the cases. Bake the cupcakes in the centre of the oven for 20–25 minutes, until an inserted skewer comes out clean. Remove from the oven and leave to cool completely.

3 To make the frosting, use an electric mixer on its fastest setting to beat the margarine until it is creamy. Sift over the icing sugar and continue to beat until well combined. Then, carefully stir in the blueberry syrup to create a smooth cream. Transfer into a piping bag with a star nozzle attached. To do this, fold over the end of the piping bag and hold the bag low down, then fill with the icing. Scrape down the contents, making sure there is no air in the bag. Pipe swirls of frosting onto the cupcakes. Decorate the swirls with blueberries. If you prefer a little less sweetness, reduce the frosting ingredients by half.

TIP:
You can also make these cupcakes with other fruits, like raspberries. Replace the blueberry syrup with raspberry syrup too.

HAZELNUT CUPCAKES
WITH CHESTNUT AND VANILLA TOPPING

Makes 12 cupcakes

Time: 40 mins prep + 25 mins baking time

For the cupcakes:

250g (9oz)	plain flour
150g (5½oz)	ground hazelnuts
200g (7oz)	fine cane sugar
1 tsp	baking powder
250ml (9fl oz)	soya milk with vanilla flavouring
120ml (4fl oz)	rapeseed oil

For the frosting:

250ml (9fl oz)	soya milk
25g (scant 1oz)	cornflour
2–3 tsp	vanilla extract
50g (1¾oz)	fine cane sugar
100g (3½oz)	soft vegan margarine, beaten until creamy
675g (1½lb)	chestnut purée
3 tbsp	rum
3–4 tbsp	icing sugar

For the filling:

250ml	carton soya cream, suitable for whipping, well chilled
1	sachet cream stiffener
100g (3½oz)	cranberry jam or hazelnut praline, plus extra for decorating
	some vanilla powder, for the nutty filling

1 Preheat the oven to 180°C (350°F/Gas 4). To make the cupcakes, combine the flour, ground hazelnuts, cane sugar, and baking powder in a bowl. In a separate bowl, whisk together the soya milk and rapeseed oil. Add the liquid ingredients to the dry ingredients and combine.

2 Put paper cases into the moulds of a muffin tray and fill evenly with the mixture. Bake the cupcakes in the centre of the oven for about 25 minutes.

3 Meanwhile, make the frosting by cooking the soya milk, cornflour, vanilla extract, and cane sugar in a pan over a moderate heat, stirring constantly until you have a custard, then leave to cool. Beat vigorously with an electric mixer, then stir in the margarine. Add the chestnut purée and rum, sift over the icing sugar, and stir everything together until you have a smooth topping.

4 For the filling – both the fruity and the nutty version – whip the cream with some cream stiffener. For the fruity version, sir in the jam; for the nutty version stir in the hazelnut praline and vanilla.

5 Use a tablespoon to scoop out a slight hole in each cake (ideally in a single piece), put in some of the filling, then pop the piece of cake you hollowed out back on top. Transfer the frosting into a piping bag with a round nozzle attached and pipe swirls on top of the cupcakes. Decorate each one with some jam or finely chopped hazelnut praline.

If you like cupcakes and strudel, you will fall in love with this exquisite creation, which combines juicy fruits, delicate spices, and soft vanilla cream.

STRUDEL CUPCAKES

Makes 12 cupcakes

Time: 35 mins + 30 mins baking

For the cupcakes:

250g (9oz)	filo pastry (ready-made; see pp.14–15)
80g (2¾oz)	vegan margarine
50g (1¾oz)	wholemeal breadcrumbs
50g (1¾oz)	fine cane sugar
500g (1lb 2oz)	apples or pears, plus extra for decorating rum (optional)

For the topping:

250ml	carton soya cream, suitable for whipping, well chilled
2	sachets cream stiffener
	seeds scraped from
1	vanilla pod
1 tsp	vanilla extract (optional)

1 For the cupcakes, first put paper cases into the moulds of a muffin tray. Cut a total of 24 squares from the filo pastry. Melt the margarine in a small pan over a moderate heat and use this to brush the pastry pieces on all sides, leaving some margarine over. In each muffin tin mould, lay 2 squares on top of one another with the points angled so that it look a bit like a star. Carefully press the pastry right down into the base and sides of each mould.

2 Preheat the oven to 180°C (350°F/Gas 4). Add half of the remaining margarine to a pan, heat it once again and sauté the breadcrumbs in it. Transfer to a bowl and mix with the sugar, then set aside. Peel and core the apples or pears and chop into little cubes. Fold the diced fruit into the breadcrumb and sugar mixture and drizzle with rum, if using.

3 Divide the fruitevenly between the muffin moulds; it is fine to pile it up a bit. Fold the corners of the pastry over the top, press down, and brush with some margarine. Bake the cupcakes in the centre of the oven for about 30 minutes, until golden brown. Remove from the oven and leave to cool completely.

4 For the topping, beat the cream with the cream stiffener, vanilla seeds, and vanilla extract, if using. Top the cupcakes with the cream and decorate with a piece of apple or pear before serving.

TIP:
To prevent the decorative fruit pieces from going brown, drizzle them with some lemon juice or brush with clear vegan jelly.

Really sinful – that's how brownies should be! Wallow in the intense chocolate flavour and creamy consistency. When combined with peanuts, the result is an unrivalled little chocolate cake.

BROWNIES WITH A PEANUT KICK

For a 20 × 20cm (8 x 8in) baking tin

Time: 30 mins prep + 45 mins baking

For the brownie mix:

100g (3½oz)	soft vegan margarine
225g (8oz)	fine cane sugar
175g (6oz)	silken tofu
150g (5½oz)	plain flour
1	seeds scraped from vanilla pod
60g (2oz)	vegan cocoa powder
1 tsp	baking powder
1	pinch of salt
60ml (2fl oz)	soya milk
8 tbsp	crunchy peanut butter
4 tbsp	maple syrup
5 tbsp	roasted peanuts
60g (2oz)	vegan dark chocolate

For the topping:

150g (5½oz)	vegan dark chocolate
1 tsp	coconut oil
3 tbsp	smooth peanut butter

1 Preheat the oven to 180°C (350°F/Gas 4). Line the baking tin with baking paper. To make the brownie mixture, beat the margarine until creamy using an electric mixer on its highest setting, gradually adding the sugar while beating. Squeeze out the silken tofu slightly and dab dry with some kitchen paper, then stir into the margarine and beat everything until you have a cohesive mixture.

2 In a separate bowl, combine the flour, vanilla seeds, cocoa powder, baking powder, and salt, then fold this into the margarine and tofu mixture. Mix the soya milk with 3 tablespoons of the crunchy peanut butter and the maple syrup and gradually stir this into the brownie mixture. Finally, chop the peanuts and dark chocolate and fold these in, too.

3 Put half the mixture into the tin and smooth it out. Then, put little blobs of the remaining crunchy peanut butter over the mixture before covering with the rest of the brownie mix. Smooth the surface and bake in the centre of the oven for about 45 minutes. Remove from the oven, leave to cool completely, and cut into 6–9 brownies.

4 Transfer the brownies to a wire rack with greaseproof paper under it. To make the topping, melt the chocolate and coconut oil over a bain-marie, stirring carefully, then spread this over the brownies. Don't worry if the chocolate runs down the sides a bit. Gently heat the smooth peanut butter and use a teaspoon to carefully make 3 little blobs, spaced slightly apart, on the still-warm chocolate. Fianlly, take a fairly thick wooden skewer and pull it through each blob to create a heart shape.

Brownies taste great when prepared American-style with lots of cocoa powder, sugar and fat, but this quickly prepared chilled version is also fantastic. Try it out some time!

RAW ALMOND BROWNIES

For a 25 × 25cm (10 x 10in) baking tin

Time: 25 mins prep + 1 day soaking + 3 hrs chilling

For the brownies:

400g (14oz)	whole almonds
100g (3½oz)	raisins
200g (7oz)	cocoa nibs (from a health food shop or organic supermarket)
100g (3½oz)	cocoa powder
4 tbsp	maple syrup
2 tbsp	baobab powder (from a health food shop, vegan supermarket, or online retailer)
6 tbsp	coconut oil

Also:

finely flaked coconut, for sprinkling

1 A day in advance, soak the almonds in plenty of water. Drain the almonds thoroughly, then grind them coarsely in a food processor. Add the remaining ingredients and process everything until you have a homogeneous mixture.

2 Sprinkle the base of the cake tin with coconut flakes. Transfer the mixture to the tin and smooth it out. Leave to stand for about 2–3 hours in the fridge, then turn it out on to a cutting board and cut into 9–12 pieces.

TIP:
If the mixture is too dry and heavy, add some more water.

CHOCOLATE CHIP COOKIES
THE SALTY WAY

Makes 10–12 cookies

75g (2½oz)	vegan margarine
75g (2½oz)	fine white cane sugar
75g (2½oz)	fine brown cane sugar
	seeds scraped from
1	vanilla pod
100g (3½oz)	plain flour
½ tsp	salt
½ tsp	bicarbonate of soda
40g (1¼oz)	ground almonds
80g (2¾oz)	vegan dark chocolate, finely chopped

Time: 20 mins prep + 10 mins baking

1 In a large bowl, beat the margarine with an electric mixer until creamy. Add the white and brown cane sugar and beat everything on the highest setting for several minutes, then stir in the vanilla seeds.

2 In a separate bowl, combine the flour, salt, bicarbonate of soda, and almonds. Gradually stir this into the fat and sugar mixture until you have a consistent dough. Finally, fold in the chocolate with a spoon so that it is evenly distributed.

3 Preheat the oven to 180°C (350°F/Gas 4). Using 2 teaspoons, cut off little portions of the dough and put them on a baking tray lined with baking paper. Take care to leave a gap between them as the dough will spread out slightly as it bakes.

4 Bake the cookies in the centre of the oven for about 10 minutes. When the edges are golden brown, remove the cookies from the oven.

TIP:

Leave the cookies to cool down completely before lifting them off the tray as they will still be very soft after baking. Cookies keep best in a tin, but even then they never stay around very long.

CREAM PUFFS
WITH CHERRY FILLING

Makes 12 small cream puffs

Time: 25 mins prep + 30 mins baking

For the cream puffs:

50g (1¾oz)	vegan margarine
150g (5½oz)	plain flour
50g (1¾oz)	cornflour
1	pinch of salt
2 tbsp	soya cream

For the filling:

350g (12oz)	jar sour cherries, drained, liquid reserved
3 tsp	vanilla extract
15g (½oz)	cornflour
250ml	carton soya cream, suitable for whipping, well chilled
1	sachet cream stiffener

1 Preheat the oven to 200°C (400°F/Gas 6). To make the cream puffs, put 250ml (9fl oz) water into a pan with the margarine and bring to the boil. Combine the flour, cornflour, and salt then add to the pan, stirring constantly with a wooden spoon. Next add the soya cream. Cook the mixture for 1–2 minutes, until it forms a smooth and supple ball and a brown coating forms on the base of the pan.

2 Transfer the ball of dough into a piping bag with a star nozzle attached. Pipe 12 spirals onto a baking tray lined with baking paper, leaving a gap between each one. Bake in the centre of the oven for 30 minutes until golden brown. Do not open the oven during baking.

3 While the cream puffs are baking, prepare the filling. Put the cherries with 100ml (3½fl oz) of the reserved marinating juice and the vanilla extract into a pan and simmer briefly. Add some of the cherry juice to the cornflour and stir until smooth, then add to the cherry mixture. Continue to simmer until the mix has begun to thicken. Remove from the hob and leave to cool. Whip the cream with the cream stiffener.

4 Remove the cream puffs from the oven, leave to cool, then slice them open with a bread knife. Spread some cherries onto the bottom halves, then add a layer of cream, and, finally, replace the tops.

TIP:

In autumn you can also make a particularly delicious filling using chestnut purée and whipped soya cream.

BERRY CRUMBLE

For a 22cm (8½in) springform tin (12 pieces)

For the base:

125g (4½oz)	spelt flour
125g (4½oz)	wholemeal spelt flour
115g (4oz)	fine cane sugar
1 tsp	baking powder
½ tsp	bicarbonate of soda
½ tsp	salt
¾ tsp	vanilla powder
1½ tbsp	chickpea flour
60ml (2fl oz)	soya milk with vanilla flavouring
60g (2oz)	soya yogurt with vanilla flavouring
3 tbsp	rapeseed oil

For the filling:

600g (1lb 5oz)	strawberries (or other berries)
1–2 tsp	vanilla extract
20g (¾oz)	fine cane sugar

For the crumble:

40g (1¼oz)	spelt flour
40g (1¼oz)	wholemeal spelt flour
½ tsp	baking powder
4 tbsp	fine cane sugar
45g (1½oz)	vegan margarine
1–2 tsp	vanilla extract
	some soya milk with vanilla flavouring

Also:

vegan vanilla ice cream or whipped soya cream, to serve

Time: 35 mins prep + 45 mins baking

1 To make the base, combine both types of spelt flour in a bowl. Add the cane sugar, baking powder, bicarbonate of soda, salt, vanilla, and chickpea flour and mix everything together thoroughly. In a separate bowl, stir the soya milk, soya yogurt, and rapeseed oil until smooth. Set both mixtures aside.

2 For the filling, trim and then halve or quarter the strawberries depending on their size. Mix with the vanilla extract and sugar and then set aside.

3 To make the crumble, combine the flours in a bowl. Mix together with the baking powder and the sugar. Work in some margarine using your fingers until the mixture is a crumbly consistency. Add the vanilla extract. If the mixture is too firm, add a bit of soya milk.

4 Preheat the oven to 180°C (350°F/Gas 4). Line the springform tin with baking paper. Combine the dry and liquid ingredient mixtures for the base until you have a smooth dough. Put three-quarters of the dough into the tin and smooth it out. Then spread the berries over the top and press down gently. Spread the remaining dough mix over the top and smooth it out again. Scatter the crumble over the top.

5 Bake the crumble cake in the centre of the oven for 40–45 minutes, until an inserted skewer comes out clean. Remove the tin from the oven and serve the crumble while still warm with vegan vanilla ice cream or chilled soya cream.

MINI PEANUT AND COCONUT CAKES
WITH CARAMEL

Makes 8 mini cakes

Time: 35 mins prep + 50 mins baking + chilling

For the mini cakes:

250g (9oz)	plain flour
225g (8oz)	fine cane sugar
1 tsp	vanilla powder
½ tsp	ground cinnamon
½ tsp	grated nutmeg
½ tsp	ground ginger
1 tsp	baking powder
1 tsp	bicarbonate of soda
1 tsp	salt
3	very ripe bananas
250ml (9fl oz)	coconut milk
120ml (4fl oz)	rapeseed oil
1 tbsp	cider vinegar

For the peanut frosting:

250g (9oz)	soft vegan margarine
300g (10oz)	smooth peanut butter
250g (9oz)	icing sugar

Also:

80g (2¾oz)	peanuts
	flaked coconut
	vegan caramel sauce (ready-made)

1 Preheat the oven to 160°C (325°F/Gas 3). For the mini cakes, combine the flour, cane sugar, vanilla, cinnamon, nutmeg, ginger, baking powder, bicarbonate of soda, and salt in a bowl. Peel the bananas and mash them to a purée with a fork. In a separate bowl, whisk the coconut milk and rapeseed oil, add the cider vinegar, and stir in the mashed bananas. Quickly stir the liquid ingredients into the dry ingredients until you have a smooth mixture, but take care not to stir too vigorously.

2 Line a 24cm (9½in) springform tin with baking paper, then transfer the mixture into the tin and smooth it out. Bake in the centre of the oven for 45–50 minutes, until an inserted skewer comes out clean. Remove from the oven and leave to cool completely. Slice the cake in half horizontally and use a glass (about 7cm/2¾in in diameter) to stamp out 16 little round cake bases.

3 For the peanut frosting, use an electric mixer on the highest setting to beat the margarine until creamy, then stir in the peanut butter. Sift over the icing sugar and, with the mixer on its lowest setting, carefully combine everything. If the frosting is too soft, simply chill it briefly.

4 Transfer the frosting into a piping bag with a round nozzle attached. Pipe blobs of the frosting mixture onto half of the little bases, then carefully put the remaining cake sections on top and finish with more generous dollops of frosting. Leave to chill. Toast the peanuts and flaked coconut in a dry pan, leave to cool, then scatter over the mini cakes. Drizzle over some caramel sauce and chill the cakes until you are ready to serve.

CAKES ETC.

Classic, mouth-watering, fruity: Essential recipes for quick, stress-free baking, exquisite coffee morning treats, and feel-good comfort food.

"BUTTER" CAKE

For a 30 x 40cm (12 x 15½in) baking tray

Time: 20 mins prep + 35 mins baking

For the cake mix:

350g (12oz)	soya cream, suitable for whipping, well chilled
200g (7oz)	fine cane sugar
1–2 tsp	vanilla extract
4 tbsp	powdered egg substitute, such as Ener-g Egg Replacer
150g (5½oz)	plain flour
150g (5½oz)	spelt flour with a high gluten content
1	pinch of salt
1 tsp	baking powder

For the topping:

175g (6oz)	vegan margarine
200g (7oz)	fine cane sugar
1–2 tsp	vanilla extract
6 tbsp	soya milk
300g (10oz)	flaked almonds

Also:

vegan margarine, for greasing the baking tray

1 Preheat the oven to 200°C (400°F/Gas 6). For the cake mix, use a balloon whisk to combine the soya cream, sugar, vanilla extract, and egg substitute until you have a smooth consistency. In a separate bowl, combine the flours, salt, and the baking powder. Beat both mixtures together until light and creamy. Spread the mixture over a well-greased baking tray and bake in the centre of the oven for 10 minutes.

2 Meanwhile, for the topping, cream the margarine with the sugar and vanilla extract. Mix in the soya milk and almonds and spread the sugar and almond mixture evenly over the pre-baked base. Cook the cake for a further 20–25 minutes, until the topping is golden brown. Remove from the oven, leave to cool, and cut into 16 pieces.

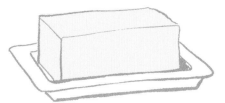

Hey presto – and it's ready! Enjoy this easy-to-make sponge cake with an attractive striped appearance.

QUICK MARBLE CAKE

For a 30cm (12in) long loaf tin

Time: 25 mins prep + 1 hr baking + 15 mins cooling

For the pale cake mix:

250g (9oz)	plain flour, plus extra for dusting
100g (3½oz)	fine cane sugar
1 tsp	bicarbonate of soda
290ml (9½fl oz)	soya milk
1	grated zest of organic lemon
150ml (5fl oz)	corn oil
2–3 tsp	vanilla extract

For the dark cake mix:

250g (9oz)	plain flour
90g (3¼oz)	fine cane sugar
1 tsp	bicarbonate of soda
25g (scant 1oz)	vegan cocoa powder
150ml (5fl oz)	corn oil
340ml (11½fl oz)	soya milk
2–3 tsp	vanilla extract

Also:

vegan margarine, for greasing the tin

1 Carefully grease a large loaf tin and dust with flour. To make the pale cake mix, combine the flour, sugar, and bicarbonate of soda in a bowl. In a separate bowl, whisk the soya milk, lemon zest, and corn oil, add the vanilla extract, then fold these into the dry ingredients. Take care not to stir too vigorously.

2 Preheat the oven to 180°C (350°F/Gas 4). For the dark cake mix, combine the flour, sugar, bicarbonate of soda, and cocoa powder. In a separate bowl whisk the corn oil and soya milk, add the vanilla extract, and fold these into the dry ingredients.

3 Put 3 tablespoons of the pale mix into the centre of the tin, then add 3 tablespoons of the dark mix on top and continue in this manner until all the cake mix has been used up. Bake the cake in the centre of the oven for 50–60 minutes, until an inserted skewer comes out clean. Leave the cake in the tin and put it on a wire rack to cool for about 15 minutes before turning it out of the tin.

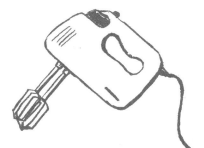

A bread or a cake? Who cares, it's fun to make, healthy, and it tastes great plain, with a dollop of soya cream, or spread with almond butter.

DELICIOUS
ALMOND BUTTER WHOLEGRAIN BREAD

For a 28cm (11in) long loaf tin

350g (12oz)	wholemeal flour, plus extra for dusting
250g (9oz)	fine cane sugar
1	pinch of salt
1	pinch of ground cinnamon
200g (7oz)	ground almonds
1½ tsp	bicarbonate of soda
1½ tsp	baking powder
60ml (2fl oz)	soya milk
1 tbsp	cider vinegar
2–3 tsp	vanilla extract
60ml (2fl oz)	almond milk
60ml (2fl oz)	rapeseed oil
5 tbsp	almond butter
1	grated zest of small organic lemon
250ml (9fl oz)	carbonated mineral water
	vegan margarine, for greasing the tin

Time: 20 mins prep + 50 mins baking + 10 mins cooling

1 Preheat the oven to 180°C (350°F/Gas 4). Combine the flour, sugar, salt, cinnamon, almonds, bicarbonate of soda, and baking powder in a bowl. In a separate bowl, whisk the soya milk with the cider vinegar, add the vanilla extract, and leave to thicken for 5 minutes. Stir in the almond milk, rapeseed oil, almond butter, and lemon zest until smooth. Quickly combine the liquid and dry ingredients with a large spoon. Then slowly add the mineral water and stir the mix again (not too vigorously) with the spoon until smooth.

2 Grease a loaf tin with margarine and dust with flour. Transfer the mixture to the tin, smooth the surface, and bake in the centre of the oven for about 50 minutes, until an inserted skewer comes out clean.

3 Remove from the oven and leave the bread to cool in the tin for about 10 minutes. Use a knife to gently loosen the loaf around the edges, knock it out of the tin, and leave to cool completely on a wire rack.

TIP:

Transform the bread into more of a cake by topping it with an almond butter and dark chocolate glaze. To do this, spread the bread with almond butter and leave to dry a little. Melt 150g (5½oz) vegan chocolate with 1 tbsp coconut oil and spread this over the almond butter layer. Optionally, toast a handful of flaked almonds in a dry pan and scatter over top.

This dark shortcrust pastry with a hint of coffee, delicious vanilla yogurt filling, and a delicate crumble is pretty hard to resist.

MARBLED CHOCOLATE CHEESECAKE

For a 22cm (8½in) springform tin

Time: 35 mins prep + 1 hr chilling + 45 mins baking

For the base:

200g (7oz)	plain flour
100g (3½oz)	fine cane sugar
2 tsp	baking powder
2 tbsp	cornflour
4 tbsp	vegan cocoa powder
1 tbsp	instant coffee granules, finely ground
1	pinch of salt
125g (4½oz)	vegan margarine
1–2 tsp	vanilla extract

For the filling:

40g (1¼oz)	cornflour
5 tbsp	soya milk with vanilla flavouring
500g (1lb 2oz)	soya yogurt with vanilla flavouring
110g (3¾oz)	fine cane sugar
1–2 tsp	vanilla extract
1	juice and zest of organic lemon
125g (4½oz)	vegan margarine

1 For the base, combine the flour, sugar, baking powder, cornflour, cocoa powder, instant coffee, and salt in a bowl. Add the margarine in little blobs and work it in with your fingers, then add the vanilla extract. If the pastry is too firm, add a few drops of water. Wrap the pastry in cling film and chill for 1 hour in the fridge.

2 Preheat the oven to 160°C (325°F/Gas 3) and line the springform tin with baking paper. Thinly cover the base of the tin with three quarters of the pastry – press it down slightly and bring up the sides so it stands about 4cm (1½in) high. Prick the pastry with a fork and chill it again.

3 To make the filling, stir together the cornflour and soya milk with a balloon whisk until smooth. Stir in the soya yogurt, sugar, vanilla extract, and lemon juice and zest. In a small pan, melt the margarine over a low heat and, when it is lukewarm (not hot), combine it with the soya and sugar cream. Spread the mixture smoothly over the pastry. From the remaining pastry, use your fingers to pull off little crumble pieces and distribute these over the filling mixture.

4 Bake in the centre of the oven for 45 minutes, until an inserted skewer comes out clean. Remove the tin from the oven and leave to cool completely.

TIP:

For a really lavish cake, double the ingredients for the topping and use a larger springform (24 or 26cm/ 8 or 10½in in diameter), and bake for about 1 hour.

DANUBE WAVE CAKES

For a 30 x 40cm (12 x 15½in) baking tray

Time: 35 mins prep + 30 mins baking

For the cake mix:

250g (9oz)	soft vegan margarine
1–2tsp	vanilla extract
250g (9oz)	fine cane sugar
500g (1lb 2oz)	plain flour
1 tsp	baking powder
4 tbsp	soya flour
300ml (10fl oz)	soya milk
4 tbsp	vegan cocoa powder
675g (1½lb)	sour cherries, pitted and drained

For the cream:

750ml (1¼ pints)	soya milk with vanilla flavouring
80g (2¾oz)	instant custard with vanilla flavouring
75g (2½oz)	fine cane sugar
250g (9oz)	soft vegan margarine

Also:

200g (7oz)	vegan dark chocolate

1 To make the cake, use an electric whisk to cream the margarine with the vanilla extract and sugar. In a separate bowl, combine the flour, baking powder, and soya flour, then fold this into the margarine and sugar mixture. Finally, stir in the soya milk.

2 Preheat the oven to 200°C (400°F/Gas 6). Spread half the mixture over a baking tray lined with baking paper. Fold the cocoa powder into the remaining mixture and spread this over the pale cake mix. Draw a fork through both mixtures to create a slightly marbled effect. Scatter the sour cherries evenly over the cake, pressing them down slightly. Bake the cake in the centre of the oven for 25–30 minutes. Remove and leave to cool completely.

3 Meanwhile, for the cream, take a few tablespoons of the soya milk and mix this with the custard powder, then stir in the sugar. Bring the remaining soya milk to the boil over a moderate heat, remove the pan from the hob, stir in the custard paste, then bring everything back to the boil, stirring constantly. Leave the custard to cool to room temperature.

4 Beat the margarine until it is fluffy, then stir in the custard a spoonful at a time. Spread this creamy mixture over the cake and smooth the surface. Melt the dark chocolate in a bain-marie, let it cool slightly, and swiftly spread it over the creamy layer. Keep the cake chilled until ready to serve, then cut into 12 pieces.

The classic German "bee sting cake" consists of a light yeast dough, a fine custard and cream filling, and a sweet layer of almonds – there is nothing else quite like it.

BEE STING CAKE

For a 30 x 40cm (12 x 15½in) baking tray

Time: 30 mins prep + 45 mins proving + 30 mins baking

For the base:

750g (1lb 10oz)	spelt flour with a high gluten content, plus extra to work with
1½	sachets dried yeast
1	pinch of salt
125g (4½oz)	fine cane sugar
100g (3½oz)	vegan margarine
200ml (7fl oz)	soya milk

For the topping:

150g (5½oz)	vegan margarine
150g (5½oz)	fine cane sugar
200g (7oz)	flaked almonds

For the filling:

300g (10oz)	rice cream, suitable for whipping, well chilled
1 litre (1¾ pints)	soya milk with vanilla flavouring
125g (4½oz)	instant custard powder
½	seeds scraped from vanilla pod
80g (2¾oz)	fine cane sugar
1	pinch of salt
20g (¾oz)	vegan margarine

1 To make the base, combine the flour, yeast, salt, and sugar in a bowl. Melt the margarine in a small pan and stir it into the dry ingredients. Then heat the soya milk and 200ml (7fl oz) water over a low heat and add these to the mix. Knead everything together until you have a smooth, supple dough. Cover the dough and leave to prove in a warm place for about 45 minutes.

2 Preheat the oven to 180°C (350°F/Gas 4). Roll out the dough and place it on a baking tray lined with baking paper.

3 To make the topping, heat the margarine with the sugar in a pan over a moderate heat, stirring constantly until melted, then mix in the flaked almonds. Spread the mixture evenly over the base using a dough scraper. Bake in the centre of the oven for 25–30 minutes. Remove from the oven and allow it to cool.

4 Meanwhile, make the filling by beating the rice cream, using an electric mixer on its highest setting, and leave to chill. Take 200ml (7fl oz) of the soya milk and stir together with the custard powder until smooth. Put the remaining soya milk, the vanilla seeds, sugar, and salt into a pan and bring to the boil over a moderate heat. Remove the pan from the hob and stir in the custard paste made earlier. Bring the mixture back to the boil, stirring constantly. Remove the pan from the hob once again and stir in the margarine. Leave the custard to cool then fold in the rice cream.

5 Once the base is cool cut it into 12 pieces. Slice each piece in half horizontally and fill with the cream.

CARROT CAKE

WITH CHOCOLATE AND CREAM CHEESE TOPPING

Here, the carrots go beautifully with the sweet white chocolate and cream cheese in the topping. Pistachios add the perfect finishing touch to the whole combination.

For a 24cm (9½in) springform tin

Time: 35 mins prep + 65 mins baking

For the cake:

400g (14oz)	plain flour
2 tsp	bicarbonate of soda
350g (12oz)	fine cane sugar
1	seeds scraped from vanilla pod
1 tsp	salt
2 tsp	ground cinnamon (slightly heaped)
2 tsp	baking powder
400g (14oz)	soya yogurt
200ml (7fl oz)	corn oil
400g (14oz)	carrots, very finely grated

For the topping:

100g (3½oz)	vegan white chocolate
80g (2¾oz)	soft vegan margarine
125g (4½oz)	vegan cream cheese
50g (1¾oz)	icing sugar
1	grated zest of organic lemon

Also:

100g (3½oz)	pistachios, chopped

1 Preheat the oven to 180°C (350°F/Gas 4). To make the cake, combine the flour, bicarbonate of soda, cane sugar, vanilla seeds, salt, and cinnamon in a medium-sized bowl. Sift in the baking powder and stir everything together again.

2 In a separate larger bowl, use a balloon whisk to mix the soya yogurt and corn oil, then vigorously stir in the grated carrot using a spoon. Add the dry ingredients in two stages, using a large spoon to mix everything to an even consistency and only stirring as much as required to combine the carrot mixture with the flour.

3 Line the springform tin with baking paper. Transfer the cake mixture into the tin and smooth the surface. Bake the cake in the centre of the oven for 65 minutes. Remove and leave to cool completely.

4 To make the topping, melt the white chocolate in a bain-marie then leave to cool to room temperature. Use an electric whisk on its fastest setting to beat the margarine and the cream cheese. Sift over the icing sugar and mix this in along with the lemon zest, using the whisk on a moderate setting. Gradually pour in the chocolate, incorporating it into the mixture with the whisk on a low setting. The result should be a smooth, creamy, soft topping, which will firm up in the fridge. Spread the topping over the carrot cake and smooth the surface. Scatter with the chopped pistachios and chill the carrot cake until ready to serve.

This gluten-free carrot cake tart contains no processed sugar and is made from raw ingredients. The base is sweetened purely using dates and the tart is finished off with a wonderfully creamy macadamia and vanilla filling.

CARROT CAKE TART
WITH MACADAMIA AND VANILLA CREAM

RAW & GLUTEN-FREE

For a 20cm (8in) springform tin (12 pieces)

Time: 20 mins prep + 12 hrs soaking + 2 hrs chilling

For the cream filling:

125g (4½oz)	macadamia nuts
80g (2¾oz)	coconut oil
3 tbsp	maple syrup
	seeds scraped from
1	vanilla pod
	juice of
½	lemon
1	pinch of salt

For the base:

3	medium carrots
90g (3¼oz)	hazelnuts
140g (5oz)	dates, pitted
40g (1¼oz)	fine coconut flakes
1	pinch of salt
1	dash grated nutmeg
1 tsp	ground cinnamon

Also:

12	macadamia nuts, for decorating

1 For the cream filling, first soak the macadamia nuts overnight in water.

2 For the base, peel and finely grate the carrots. Use a food processor to finely chop the hazelnuts and dates. Add the coconut flakes, salt, nutmeg, and cinnamon and process everything until you have a smooth paste. Mix in the grated carrot. Transfer the mixture to a springform tin lined with baking paper, press the mixture down slightly and use your fingers to press up the sides until you have an edge that is about 2cm (¾in) high. Refrigerate.

3 Meanwhile, to make the cream filling, melt the coconut oil in a small pan over a low heat. Drain the macadamia nuts and blend them in a food processor with the coconut oil, maple syrup, vanilla seeds, lemon juice, salt, and 60ml (2fl oz) water until you have a delicious, smooth cream. Spread the cream over the base, smooth the surface, and chill the cake in the fridge for at least 2 hours. Garnish with macadamia nuts.

This sweet flower always creates a bit of a sensation at
the breakfast table or at a picnic with friends.

SWEET RASPBERRY FLOWER

For a 30cm (12in) springform tin (16 pieces)

Time: 35 mins prep + 55 mins proving + 30 mins baking

For the dough:

1	cube fresh yeast
50g (1¾oz)	vegan margarine
600g (1lb 5oz)	spelt flour, plus extra for dusting
100g (3½oz)	fine cane sugar
2 tsp	salt

For the filling:

300g (10oz)	raspberries (frozen)
20g (¾oz)	fine cane sugar
50g (1¾oz)	flaked almonds
2	mint leaves

1 To make the dough, put 300ml (10fl oz) lukewarm water into a bowl and crumble in the yeast. Cover and leave to prove at room temperature for about 10 minutes, then use a balloon whisk to mix to a smooth consistency. Melt the margarine in a small pan over a low heat. Combine the flour, sugar, and salt in a bowl.

2 Add the water and yeast mixture to the dry ingredients along with the margarine, and knead everything to create a smooth dough. Cover and leave to prove in a warm place until it has doubled in size.

3 Meanwhile, for the filling, heat the raspberries with the sugar over a low heat. Purée, leave to cool briefly, then fold in the almonds. Finely chop the mint leaves and add these, too.

4 Knead the dough through once more and divide into 3 equal-sized portions. Roll these out on a floured work surface to create roughly 1cm (½in) thick discs with a diameter of about 30cm (12in). Place the first disc into the springform tin, cover it with half the raspberry and almond mixture, then place the second disc on top and cover with the remaining raspberry and almond mixture. Place the third disc of dough on top to form the final layer – this does not get a raspberry topping.

5 Preheat the oven to 180°C (350°F/Gas 4). Use a glass (about 8cm/¾in in diameter) to create an indentation in the centre of the dough disc. Cut the dough just as far as this glass indentation to create 16 equal sections. Now take hold of each piece (grasping the top and bottom layers together) and twist it 3 times. Finally, fold over the outer edges of 2 adjacent pieces, shaping them to be nice and round, and join them together to create a "flower petal". Repeat to create 7 more petals. Bake the flower in the centre of the oven for 30 minutes.

BANANA BREAD

For a 28cm (11in) long loaf tin

Time: 20 mins prep + 1 hr baking

For the dough:

300g (10oz)	plain flour, plus extra for dusting
2 tbsp	cornflour
1 heaped tsp	baking powder
1¼ tsp	bicarbonate of soda
½ tsp	salt
250g (9oz)	fine cane sugar
1 tsp	vanilla powder
½ tsp	ground cinnamon
¼ tsp	grated nutmeg
100ml (3½fl oz)	soya milk
75ml (2½fl oz)	rapeseed oil
200g (7oz)	vegan sour cream (or soya yogurt with a squeeze of lemon)
4	medium, very ripe bananas

Also:

vegan margarine, for greasing the tin
icing sugar, for dusting

1 Preheat the oven to 180°C (350°F/Gas 4). In a large bowl, combine the flour, cornflour, baking powder, bicarbonate of soda, salt, cane sugar, vanilla, cinnamon, and nutmeg.

2 In a separate bowl, stir the soya milk with the rapeseed oil and sour cream until smooth. Peel the bananas and mash well with a fork until you have a creamy mixture with an even consistency. Stir the banana purée into the soya milk mixture. Quickly stir together the liquid and dry ingredients with a spoon until there are no lumps in the mix.

3 Grease a loaf tin with margarine and dust with flour. Transfer the mixture to the tin, smooth the surface, and bake the bread in the centre of the oven for 50–60 minutes, until an inserted skewer comes out clean.

TIP:

Banana bread tastes great plain or spread with some vegan margarine. To decorate, you can also make an icing by stirring together some icing sugar and banana juice. Spread this on top of the bread and scatter over some chopped banana chips to decorate.

Chocolate lovers and fruit fans both get their money's worth here. This chocolate cake can be made with almost any type of fruit or berries. Enveloped in a delicate chocolate glaze and topped with toasted almonds, this is a truly special creation.

CHOCOLATEY FRUIT CAKE

For a 23 × 23cm (9 x9in) baking tin

For the cake:

500g (1lb 2oz)	seasonal fruit
470ml (15½fl oz)	soya milk
3 tsp	cider vinegar
200g (7oz)	fine cane sugar
1–2 tsp	vanilla extract
270g (9½oz)	wholemeal spelt flour
60g (2oz)	vegan cocoa powder, sifted
1½ tsp	bicarbonate of soda
1 tsp	baking powder
½ tsp	salt
130ml (4½fl oz)	sunflower oil

Also:

150g (5½oz)	vegan dark chocolate
1 tbsp	coconut oil
	flaked almonds, for scattering

Time: 30 mins prep + 40 mins baking

1 Preheat the oven to 180°C (350°F/Gas 4). To make the cake, first chop the fruit into pieces. In a bowl, whisk the soya milk with the cider vinegar and leave to thicken for 5 minutes. Stir in the sugar and vanilla extract with a balloon whisk. In a separate bowl, combine the flour, cocoa powder, bicarbonate of soda, baking powder, and salt. Fold the dry ingredients into the liquid mixture and combine until you have a smooth consistency. Next, stir in the sunflower oil and combine well with the mixture. Finally fold in the fruit.

2 Transfer the mixture to a tin lined with baking paper, smooth the surface, and bake in the centre of the oven for about 40 minutes, until an inserted skewer comes out clean. Remove and leave to cool completely.

3 Melt the chocolate with the coconut oil in a bain-marie, stir until smooth, and cover the cake all over. Carefully toast the flaked almonds in a dry pan and scatter them over the still molten chocolate. Slice the cake into about 16 pieces to serve.

TIP:
It is important to wash and chop the fresh fruit at the start, because the mix shouldn't be left to stand for too long. If you use tinned or frozen fruit, this will need to be thoroughly drained or squeezed so the cake doesn't go soggy. If necessary, reduce the quantity of fruit slightly.

Juicy pears on a pale base, covered with a delicate marzipan crumble – a really luxurious tray bake!

PEAR CAKE
WITH MARZIPAN CRUMBLE

For a 30 x 40cm (12 x 15½in) baking tray

Time: 40 mins prep + 1 hr proving + 50 mins baking

For the filling:

1.5kg (3lb 3oz)	pears
4 tbsp	fine cane sugar
2–3 tsp	vanilla extract

For the base:

400g (14oz)	spelt flour
90g (3¼oz)	fine cane sugar
1	pinch of salt
200ml (7fl oz)	soya milk
1–2 tsp	vanilla extract
½	cube fresh yeast
80g (2¾oz)	vegan margarine

For the marzipan crumble:

180g (6¼oz)	spelt flour
3 tbsp	cane sugar
100g (3½oz)	vegan margarine
200g (7oz)	marzipan
1–2 tsp	vanilla extract

1 Prepare the filling by peeling and quartering the pears, then remove the cores and chop the pears into cubes. Place the fruit in a pan, add the sugar and vanilla extract, and cook for 8–10 minutes over a moderate heat initially, then reducing to a low heat. Leave to cool.

2 For the base, combine the flour, sugar, and salt in a bowl. Gently heat the soya milk in a small pan over a low heat and add the vanilla extract. Pour this into a separate bowl, finely crumble the yeast into the milk, and leave to stand for about 10 minutes.

3 In the meantime, add blobs of the margarine to the flour mixture and swiftly work them in until the flour has completely absorbed the fat. Stir the milk and yeast mixture until smooth, then knead this in; the yeast dough should be nice and smooth. Cover and leave to prove in a warm place for about 30 minutes.

4 Line a baking tray with baking paper and roll the dough out on it, creating a slight rim around the edge. Leave the dough to prove for about 20 minutes.

5 Preheat the oven to 180°C (350°F/Gas 4). To make the crumble, mix the flour with the sugar. Add the margarine, and marzipan in little pieces, working them in with your fingers to create a crumbly texture. Add the vanilla extract. Spread the pear compote evenly over the base. Scatter the crumble over the filling and bake the cake in the centre of the oven for 40–50 minutes. Remove from the oven and leave to cool. Cut into 12 pieces.

TIP:

Try sprinkling with icing sugar to serve. This cake tastes delicious served warm with some vegan vanilla ice cream.

PEAR JUICE TART
WITH CINNAMON CREAM

For a 26cm (10½in) springform tin (12 pieces)

For the base:

250g (9oz)	plain flour
125g (4½oz)	fine cane sugar
½ tsp	baking powder
150g (5½oz)	vegan margarine
1–2 tsp	vanilla extract

For the filling:

800g (1¾lb)	pears
900ml (1½ pints)	pear juice
85g (3oz)	cornflour
6 tbsp	fine cane sugar
1–2 tsp	vanilla extract

Also:

250ml	carton soya cream, suitable for whipping, well chilled
	ground cinnamon, for dusting

Time: 40 mins prep + 1 hr chilling + 1 hr baking

1 To make the base, combine the flour, sugar, and baking powder in a bowl. Work in the margarine using your fingers, add the vanilla extract, and bring everything together to create a smooth shortcrust pastry. Line a springform tin with baking paper. Put the pastry into the tin, pressing it down and smoothing it out with a tablespoon. Create a rim of 7cm (2¾in) up the sides. Prick the base with a fork and leave to chill for 1 hour.

2 Meanwhile, to make the filling, peel and quarter the pears, remove the cores, and dice the pears finely. Put the pear juice into a pan. In a bowl, mix the cornflour with the sugar, add a bit of the pear juice and vanilla extract, and stir until the mixture is smooth and there are no visible lumps.

3 Preheat the oven to 180°C (350°F/Gas 4). Bring the pear juice to the boil over a moderate heat, remove the pan from the hob, and stir in the cornflour mixture. Bring the mixture back to the boil, stirring constantly, then swiftly fold in the diced pear. Pour over the shortcrust base and bake the tart in the centre of the oven for 1 hour. Remove and leave to cool completely in the tin.

4 Whip the soya cream and then chill until ready to serve. Cut the tart into pieces, put a generous blob of cream on each portion, and dust with plenty of cinnamon.

TIP:
This recipe also tastes fantastic made with apples and apple juice. Drizzle the diced fruit with lemon juice to prevent it going brown.

APRICOT STRUDEL TART
WITH ALMONDS AND SESAME SEEDS

For a 24cm (9½in) springform tin (12–14 pieces)

Time: 40 mins prep + 35 mins baking

For the strudel tart:

1	pack filo pastry (10 sheets, measuring 30 × 30cm/12 x 12in)
10	apricots
400g (14oz)	apples
60g (2oz)	vegan margarine
100g (3½oz)	wholemeal breadcrumbs
25g (scant 1oz)	cane sugar
1–2 tsp	vanilla extract
50g (1¾oz)	chopped almonds
25g (scant 1oz)	sesame seeds
50g (1¾oz)	ground almonds
1 tsp	ground cinnamon
½ tsp	ground cardamom
1	pinch of ground ginger
5 tbsp	maple syrup

Also:

25g (scant 1oz)	sesame seeds
25g (scant 1oz)	flaked almonds
3 tbsp	maple syrup

1 Remove the filo pastry from the fridge 10 minutes before preparation.

2 Preheat the oven to 180°C (350°F/Gas 4). Halve, stone, and dice the apricots. Peel, core, and finely dice the apples. Melt 2 tbsp margarine in a pan over a moderate heat and toast the breadcrumbs in the fat. Stir in the sugar and vanilla extract. Briefly cook the chopped almonds with the sesame seeds in a dry pan until pale brown. Combine these with the ground almonds. Mix the cinnamon with the cardamom and ginger. Melt the remaining margarine.

3 Place 2 sheets of filo on top of each other, brush with a thin layer of margarine, top with one fifth each of the fruit, breadcrumbs, almond and sesame seed mixture, and the spices. As you work, leave a gap of about 3cm (1½in) free around the edges. Finally, drizzle with 1 tablespoon maple syrup. Fold in the sides and roll up the strudel lengthways. Repeat four more times with the remaining ingredients.

4 Line a springform tin with baking paper and place the strudels inside, one beside the other in a spiral formation (it doesn't matter if the filo tears a bit at the top). Finally, brush the strudel tart with margarine.

5 Toast the sesame seeds and flaked almonds in a dry pan and scatter them over the strudel tart. Drizzle with maple syrup, and bake in the centre of the oven for 35 minutes. Remove and leave to cool completely.

TIP:

Optionally, take 500ml (16fl oz) well-chilled soya cream, suitable for whipping, add 2 sachets of cream stiffener and 2 tsp ground vanilla then beat with an electric whisk for 3 minutes until stiff. Spread over the tart.

Fruity on the bottom, fluffy on the top: this moist poppy seed and redcurrant cake is topped with a vegan version of fluffy meringue. This cake looks absolutely stunning.

POPPY SEED AND REDCURRANT CAKE
WITH A MERINGUE TOPPING

For a 30 x 40cm (12 x 15½in) baking tray

Time: 40 mins prep + 40 mins baking

For the cake:

350g (12oz)	wholemeal flour
1 tbsp	cornflour
1	slightly heaped tsp baking powder
1 tsp	(slightly heaped) bicarbonate of soda
70g (2¼oz)	ground poppy seeds
225g (8oz)	fine cane sugar
2 tsp	vanilla powder
250ml (9fl oz)	soya milk
1 tbsp	cider vinegar
110ml (3¾fl oz)	rapeseed oil
350g (12oz)	redcurrants

For the meringue topping:

2 tbsp	powdered egg substitue, such as Ener-g egg Egg Replacer
250g (9oz)	fine cane sugar
1 tbsp	agar-agar
1	generous splash rum
	some icing sugar, for dusting

1 Preheat the oven to 180°C (350°F/Gas 4). To make the cake, combine the dry ingredients in a large bowl. In a separate bowl, whisk the soya milk with the cider vinegar and leave to thicken for 5 minutes. Add the rapeseed oil and 175ml (6fl oz) water and whisk everything together. Stir the liquid mixture into the dry ingredients – a couple of lumps here and there won't matter.

2 Line a high-sided baking tray with baking paper. Smooth the cake mixture out over the tray. Scatter the redcurrants over and press them down slightly. Bake the cake in the centre of the oven for 30–40 minutes, until an inserted skewer comes out clean. Remove and leave to cool completely.

3 Preheat the oven to 240°C (475°F/Gas 9) with the grill setting enabled. To make the meringue, put the egg substitute and 300ml (10fl oz) water into a container and beat with an electric mixer on its highest setting for 5 minutes, then sprinkle in 150g (5½oz) of the sugar and continue to beat.

4 In a pan bring 200ml (7fl oz) water to the boil with the remaining 100g (3½oz) sugar and the agar-agar, stirring constantly, then add the rum. As soon as the sugar has dissolved, stir this quickly into the meringue mixture.

5 Spread the mixture over the cake, shaping it into waves and dusting with icing sugar. Cook the cake for 1–2 minutes under the grill until the topping has browned slightly. Remove from the oven, leave to cool, and refrigerate. To serve, slice into 12 pieces.

TIP:
Keep a very close eye on the cake while it's under the grill – meringue burns very easily! For a less sweet version, simply halve the meringue ingredients.

This fruity treat is topped with an exquisite creamy layer of icing and delicate flowers. It looks impressive, but is super quick to make.

RASPBERRY AND GOOSEBERRY CAKE

For a 23 × 23cm (9 x 9in) square springform tin

Time: 40 mins prep + 40 mins baking

For the cake:

3 tbsp	rapeseed oil
100g (3½oz)	chickpea flour
190g (6½oz)	icing sugar
200g (7oz)	plain flour
2 tsp	baking powder
1 tsp	bicarbonate of soda
1 tsp	vanilla powder
1	pinch of salt
2 tsp	cider vinegar
85ml (2¾fl oz)	soya milk
150g (5½oz)	raspberries
100g (3½oz)	gooseberries

For the topping:

40g (1¼oz)	cornflour
½ tsp	ground vanilla
250ml (9fl oz)	raspberry juice (online)
150g (5½oz)	soft vegan margarine
40g (1¼oz)	icing sugar
	edible flowers, such as pink and white daisies, for decorating (optional)

TIP:

Lots of other seasonal berries will also taste great – you could try combining the raspberries with blackcurrants.

1 Preheat the oven to 180°C (350°F/Gas 4). Line a square springform tin with baking paper. To make the cake, whisk the rapeseed oil with 150ml (5fl oz) water in a bowl, then use an electric whisk to beat in the chickpea flour. Add the icing sugar with the whisk on its highest setting.

2 In a separate bowl, combine the plain flour, baking powder, bicarbonate of soda, vanilla, and salt. Stir this into the chickpea mix by the spoonful, then swiftly combine everything with the spoon until smooth.

3 Stir the cider vinegar into the soya milk, leave to thicken for about 5 minutes, stir it all through again, then fold into the cake mix using a spoon. Transfer the mixture into the tin and smooth the surface. Mix the berries and scatter them over the cake, pressing down slightly. Bake in the centre of the oven for about 40 minutes, until an inserted skewer comes out clean. Remove and leave to cool completely.

4 To make the icing, combine the cornflour with the vanilla in a pan. Stir in the raspberry juice until smooth and bring to the boil over a moderate heat, stirring constantly. As soon as the mixture has thickened, remove the pan from the heat and allow the mixture to cool to room temperature, stirring occasionally.

5 Use an electric whisk on its highest setting to cream the margarine in a bowl. Sift over the icing sugar and mix it in with the whisk on a moderate setting. Then fold the vanilla and raspberry cream into the margarine and sugar mixture, one spoonful at a time. Stir it all together until smooth then spread over the cake. If desired, decorate the cake with edible flowers, before slicing into 12 pieces.

These lovely cream-filled double biscuits are vegan – so they don't just play a supporting role in this "cheesecake", they are given star billing.

OREO "CHEESECAKE"

For a 24cm (9½in) springform tin (12 pieces)

For the filling:

1kg (2¼lb)	soya yogurt
1	juice and zest of organic lemon
3½ tbsp	rapeseed oil
120ml (4fl oz)	soya milk
70g (2¼oz)	cornflour
150g (5⅕oz)	fine cane sugar
1	pinch of salt
1 tsp	vanilla powder (or the seeds from
1	vanilla pod)

For the base:

60g (2oz)	vegan margarine
16	Oreo cookies, plus
4	cookies reserved for decoration

Time: 35 mins prep + 12 hrs draining + 2 hrs cooling and baking

1 Line a sieve with a clean tea towel and place it over a large bowl. Pour in the soya yogurt and leave to drain overnight. The following day, squeeze out any excess water from the yogurt.

2 To make the base, melt the margarine in a pan over a low heat. Use a food processor to blitz the Oreo cookies to make crumbs. Gradually add the margarine and work until everything is combined. Line a springform tin with baking paper. Cover the base with a thin layer of the cookie mixture, press it down slightly with a spoon, and smooth the surface. Leave to chill in the fridge for at least 1 hour.

3 Preheat the oven to 180°C (350°F/Gas 4). To make the filling, put the soya yogurt into a bowl and stir in the lemon juice, lemon zest, and rapeseed oil until smooth. In a separate bowl, stir the soya milk and cornflour until smooth, then mix in the sugar, salt, and the vanilla. Finally, stir everything into the soya yogurt and lemon mixture until you have a smooth and creamy consistency. Spread this mixture over the biscuit base.

4 Carefully twist apart the 2 layers of the Oreo cookies you saved for decoration and arrange them on the cheesecake, creamy side down, pressing them slightly into the mixture. Bake in the centre of the oven for 50–60 minutes. Remove from the oven, leave to cool slightly, then transfer to the fridge to cool completely.

"CHEESECAKE" WITH MANGO CREAM

For a 28cm (11in) springform tin (12–14 pieces)

Time: 20 mins prep + 3 hrs chilling

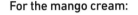

For the base:

2 tbsp	coconut oil
200g (7oz)	cashew nuts
150g (5½oz)	macadamia nuts
100g (3½oz)	fine coconut flakes
1 tbsp	lemon juice
1 tsp	grated organic lemon zest
1 tbsp	agave syrup
1	pinch of salt

For the filling:

150g (5½oz)	coconut oil
750g (1lb 10oz)	cashew nuts
150ml (5fl oz)	lemon juice
85ml (2¾fl oz)	agave syrup
½	seeds scraped from vanilla pod

For the mango cream:

300g (10oz)	mango chips, plus extra for decorating (from an organic or health food shop)
1 tbsp	psyllium husks
2 tbsp	agave syrup
1 tbsp	lemon juice

1 Melt the coconut oil for both the base and the filling in a small pan over a low heat. To make the base, finely grind the cashew and macadamia nuts in a food processor. Add 2 tablespoons coconut oil and the remaining base ingredients, plus the salt and process everything until you have a homogeneous mixture. Transfer to a springform tin lined with baking paper, smooth the surface, then chill for 30 minutes.

2 To make the filling, combine the remaining coconut oil with the other ingredients in a food processor on its top setting until it forms a well-combined, smooth paste. If this is too thick, add a bit of water and mix again. Spread the filling over the base and transfer to the freezer for 30 minutes.

3 In the meantime, make the mango cream by mixing all the ingredients in a food processor on its highest setting until you have a smooth consistency. Spread this quickly over the frozen surface of the cheesecake (it will set rapidly). Put the cheesecake in the fridge for at least 2 hours and scatter with mango chips before serving.

TIP:
If you are short of time, you can simply put the cheesecake in the freezer for 1 hour before serving.

83

ALMOND "CHEESECAKE"
WITH BLUEBERRIES

For a 24cm (9½in) springform tin (12–14 pieces)

Time: 45 mins prep + 70 mins baking + at least 1 hr chilling

For the base:

250g (9oz)	plain flour
½ tsp	baking powder
125g (4½oz)	fine cane sugar
150g (5½oz)	vegan margarine, chilled
1–2 tsp	vanilla extract

For the filling:

350g (12oz)	blanched whole almonds (alternatively, ground almonds)
500g (1lb 2oz)	soya yogurt
200g (7oz)	fine cane sugar
1–2 tsp	vanilla extract
2	juice and zest of organic lemons
80g (2¾oz)	cornflour
175ml (6fl oz)	almond milk
125g (4½oz)	coconut oil
250g (9oz)	blueberries

Also:

1	sachet clear cake glaze, vegan
50g (1¾oz)	fine cane sugar

1 To make the base, combine the flour, baking powder, and sugar in a bowl. Add the margarine and vanilla extract and use your fingers to quickly work the ingredients to create a smooth shortcrust texture. Transfer to a springform tin lined with baking paper, making sure the pastry comes about 7cm (2¾in) up the sides. Prick the base with a fork and leave to chill.

2 Preheat the oven to 180°C (350°F). For the filling, finely grind the almonds in a food processor on its highest setting. Mix the almonds, soya yogurt, sugar, vanilla extract, and lemon juice and zest and leave to rest briefly. Stir the cornflour into the almond milk until smooth and add this to the main mixture.

3 Melt the coconut oil in a small pan over a low heat. Then swiftly stir it into the almond and yogurt mixture with a balloon whisk and pour this into your shortcrust base. Bake the cheesecake in the centre of the oven for 70 minutes. Remove from the oven and leave to cool for about an hour.

4 Top the "cheesecake" with the blueberries. In a saucepan, mix the cake glaze with the sugar and 250ml (9fl oz) cold water, stirring until smooth. Bring briefly to the boil and let it cool slightly while stirring. Then carefully distribute it over the blueberries using a spoon. The cheesecake tastes best if the flavours are left to develop overnight.

TIP:

You can also use frozen blueberries instead of fresh. To make sure the filling doesn't go soggy, you should spread 2 tbsp vegan cream stiffener over the surface before you add the berries.

SWISS ROLL
WITH RASPBERRY CREAM

Makes 1 Swiss roll (10–12 pieces)

Time: 30 mins prep + 15 mins baking

For the sponge mix:

225g (8oz)	plain flour
2 tbsp	cornflour
1 tsp	baking powder
150g (5½oz)	soya yogurt with vanilla flavouring
100ml (3½fl oz)	soya milk
4 tbsp	soya flour
2 tbsp	rapeseed oil
150g (5½oz)	fine cane sugar, plus extra for sprinkling

For the raspberry cream:

200g (7oz)	soya cream, suitable for whipping, well chilled
1	sachet cream stiffener
150g (5½oz)	soya yogurt with vanilla flavouring
150g (5½oz)	raspberries

Also:

icing sugar, for dusting

1 Preheat the oven to 180°C (350°F/Gas 4) and line a baking tray with baking paper. To make the sponge for the Swiss roll, sift the flour, cornflour, and baking powder into a large bowl. In a separate bowl, stir together the soya yogurt, soya milk, soya flour, rapeseed oil, and cane sugar until the sugar has dissolved as much as possible. Stir the liquid ingredients into the dry ingredients and spread the mixture over the baking paper. Bake the sponge in the centre of the oven for 12–15 minutes.

2 In the meantime, sprinkle sugar over a clean tea towel. Turn the sponge out onto the towel while it is still hot and carefully pull off the baking paper. Use the towel to carefully roll up the sponge to create a Swiss roll shape, then leave to cool completely.

3 To make the raspberry cream, whip the soya cream using an electric mixer on its highest setting for at least 3 minutes, gradually adding the cream stiffener at the end as you whisk. Then stir in the soya yogurt. Carefully fold in the raspberries and leave to chill briefly. Unroll the sponge and spread with the raspberry cream, leaving a 2cm (¾in) gap around the edges. Then roll it up again and refrigerate. Serve dusted with icing sugar.

TIP:

If you prefer a firmer consistency for your cream filling, let the yogurt drain overnight in a sieve lined with a tea towel. The resulting "cheese" can be folded into the soya cream, as described above.

CAKES AND TARTS

Impressive dishes for guests and parties: exquisite creamy creations to enchant your friends, eye-catching festive treats, and surprise birthday cakes.

This edible "molehill" has a dark base, lots of cream, shards of chocolate, and a sweet little mound of cream covered in large crumble pieces.

MOLEHILL CAKE

For a 24cm (9½in) springform tin (12 pieces)

Time: 35 mins prep + 40 mins baking + at least 13 hrs chilling

For the crumble:

300g (10oz)	plain flour
150g (5½oz)	fine cane sugar
1 tbsp	vegan cocoa powder, sifted
150g (5½oz)	vegan margarine
1 tsp	vanilla extract

For the base:

150g (5½oz)	plain flour
2 tbsp	cornflour
125g (4½oz)	icing sugar, sifted
1 tbsp	vegan cocoa powder, sifted
1½ tsp	baking powder
½ tsp	vanilla powder
1	pinch of salt
120ml (4fl oz)	soya milk
5 tbsp	rapeseed oil

For the filling:

2 x 250ml	cartons soya cream, suitable for whipping, well chilled
2	sachets cream stiffener
6	medium bananas
80g (2¾oz)	vegan dark chocolate
3 tbsp	apricot jam

1 Preheat the oven to 180°C (350°F/Gas 4). To make the crumble, combine the flour, cane sugar, and cocoa powder in a bowl. Add the margarine in blobs with the vanilla extract and work into the mix with your fingers to create a rough crumble. Spread the crumble over a baking tray lined with baking paper, and bake in the centre of the oven for about 20 minutes.

2 For the base, combine the flour, cornflour, icing sugar, cocoa powder, baking powder, vanilla, and salt in a bowl. In a separate bowl, whisk the soya milk and rapeseed oil. Stir the liquid and dry ingredients together quickly with a large spoon. Line a springform tin with baking paper, spoon in the mixture, smooth the surface, and bake in the centre of the oven for about 20 minutes, until an inserted skewer comes out clean. Remove from the oven and leave to cool completely.

3 Meanwhile, for the filling, beat the soya cream with an electric whisk on its highest setting; after about 2 minutes add the cream stiffener and continue to beat for a further 2–3 minutes. Peel 3 of the bananas, mash them to a pulp with a fork, and fold into the cream. Chop the dark chocolate, fold this into the banana and cream mixture, and transfer to the fridge to chill for at least 1 hour.

4 Gently heat the apricot jam in a small pan over a low heat and spread it over the base of the cake. Peel the remaining bananas, slice into discs, and place them on the base. Spread the banana cream over the top and return the cake to the fridge to chill for a few minutes. Cover the creamy topping with crumble pieces and leave the cake to firm up in the fridge overnight.

TIP:
You can also make the crumble finer and pile up the cream in a dome shape on top of the cake to make it look even more like a molehill.

BANANA CAKE
WITH SOUR CREAM AND CHOCOLATE FROSTING

For a 24cm (9½in) springform tin (12–14 pieces)

Time: 45 mins prep + 1 hr baking + 12 hrs chilling

For the cake:

450g (1lb)	plain flour
1 tsp	baking powder
250g (9oz)	fine cane sugar
1 tsp	vanilla powder
2 tbsp	cornflour
	lemon zest
100ml (3½fl oz)	corn oil
100ml (3½fl oz)	rice milk
350ml (12fl oz)	carbonated mineral water

For the frosting:

350g (12oz)	vegan dark chocolate
115g (4oz)	vegan margarine
½ tsp	vanilla powder
300g (10oz)	vegan sour cream (at room temperature)
750g (1lb 10oz)	icing sugar

For the filling and decoration:

5	medium bananas
	rum
	dark and white vegan chocolate, grated (optional)

1 Preheat the oven to 180°C (350°F/Gas 4). For the cake, combine the flour, baking powder, cane sugar, vanilla, cornflour, and lemon zest. Whisk the corn oil with the rice milk and add to the dry ingredients. Slowly stir in the mineral water with a spoon until all the lumps in the mixture have gone.

2 Line a springform tin with baking paper, put the mixture into the tin, and bake in the centre of the oven for about 1 hour. When an inserted skewer comes out clean, the cake is ready. Leave to cool completely.

3 To make the frosting, break the chocolate into pieces and melt with the margarine in a bain-marie. Stir the vanilla into the sour cream and fold this into the chocolate mixture. Sift over the icing sugar and mix it in with an electric whisk. Slice the cake horizontally into 3 layers. Place one of the pieces on a cake plate, put a cake ring around it and spread with a thin layer of the frosting.

4 Peel the bananas for the filling and slice thinly. Distribute half of the slices over the frosting and press down slightly. Place the second cake layer on top and drizzle with rum. Cover with a thin layer of frosting and top with sliced banana. Put the third cake layer on top and likewise drizzle with rum before spreading over the frosting. Run a knife between the edge of the cake and the ring to release it. Cover the sides of the cake with the remaining frosting and decorate the cake with grated chocolate, if using. Ideally, put it in the fridge overnight to let the flavours develop.

A cake for special occasions and courageous bakers! A bit of effort is required here, but it is well worth it. Make sure you invite some friends over to eat it, or hold a party as soon as the cake is ready!

NEAPOLITAN WAFER CAKE

For two 24cm (9½in) springform tins (12 pieces)

Time: 45 mins prep + 40 mins baking + at least 12 hrs chilling

For the cake layers:

500g (1lb 2oz)	plain flour
300g (10oz)	ground hazelnuts
400g (14oz)	fine cane sugar
30g (1oz)	baking powder
1 tsp	ground vanilla
500ml (16fl oz)	soya milk with vanilla flavouring
240ml (8fl oz)	rapeseed oil

For the filling:

1.2 litres (2 pints)	soya cream, suitable for whipping, well chilled
4	packs of Neapolitan wafer biscuits (each weighing 75g/2½oz)
100g (3½oz)	apricot jam

Also:

1	pack Neapolitan wafers
50g (1¾oz)	vegan dark chocolate, melted

1 Preheat the oven to 180°C (350°F). For the cake layers, combine the flour, hazelnuts, sugar, baking powder, and vanilla in a bowl. In a separate bowl, mix the soya milk and rapeseed oil, then stir these into the dry ingredients until thoroughly combined. Line 2 springform tins with baking paper and put half the mixture into each. Bake in the centre of the oven for about 40 minutes, until an inserted skewer comes out clean. Remove from the oven and leave to cool completely.

2 For the filling, whip the cream, with an electric whisk on its highest setting, for at least 3 minutes until stiff. Put the Neapolitan wafers into a freezer bag and bash them with a rolling pin to create fine crumbs. Gradually fold the crumbs into the cream, then whisk on the highest setting until well combined. Refrigerate.

3 Slice both of the cakes horizontally with a sharp knife or cheese wire to create 4 cake sections. Place one of these sections on a cake platter. Heat the apricot jam in a small pan, then spread a quarter of it on the cake followed by a quarter of the cream, smoothing the surface to finish. Continue layering up cake, jam, and cream in this manner with the remaining sections finishing with a mound of cream on top.

4 To decorate, chop the Neapolitan wafers into pieces and scatter them over the centre of the cake, then drizzle with melted chocolate. Put the cake in the fridge and leave the flavours to develop overnight.

TIP:
If you'd like the cake to be even nuttier and sweeter, replace the apricot jam with vegan hazelnut spread.

FRANKFURT CROWN CAKE

For one 26cm (10½in) diameter ring mould

Time: 25 mins prep + 70 mins baking + at least 2 hrs chilling

For the cake:

600g (1lb 5oz)	plain flour, plus extra for dusting
350g (12oz)	fine cane sugar
2 tsp	baking powder
1–2	grated zest of organic lemons
1 tsp	salt
300ml (10fl oz)	rapeseed oil
525ml (17fl oz)	carbonated mineral water
	vegan margarine, for greasing the mould

For the buttercream:

500ml (16fl oz)	vegan hazelnut drink
40g (1¼oz)	instant custard powder
75g (2½oz)	fine cane sugar
250g (9oz)	soft vegan margarine
200ml (7fl oz)	soya cream, suitable for whipping

For the praline:

10g (¼oz)	vegan margarine
50g (1¾oz)	fine cane sugar
125g (4½oz)	chopped almonds

Also:

3 tbsp	cherry jam
12	glacé cherries

1 Preheat the oven to 180°C (350°C/Gas 4). To make the cake, combine the flour, sugar, baking powder, lemon zest, and salt. Use a large spoon to quickly stir in the rapeseed oil, then add the mineral water until you have a homogeneous mixture. Grease a ring mould with margarine and dust with flour. Transfer the cake mix into the tin and bake in the centre of the oven for 70 minutes, until an inserted skewer comes out clean.

2 Meanwhile, for the buttercream, measure out about 150ml (5fl oz) of the hazelnut drink and stir in the custard powder and sugar until smooth. Bring the rest of the drink to the boil in a pan over a moderate heat. Remove from the hob, stir in the custard powder mixture, then bring everything back to the boil before leaving to cool, stirring occasionally. Cream the margarine until light and fluffy and fold it into the custard spoon by spoon. Whip the cream and fold this into the mixture.

3 For the praline, melt the margarine in a pan, add the sugar and let this dissolve, then cook until it turns brown. Stir in the almonds. Spread the mixture out over baking paper and leave to cool, then crumble it up to create your praline. Press the cherry jam through a sieve and stir until smooth.

4 Turn the cake out from the tin and slice it to create 3 layers. Spread the bottom section with cherry jam and cover this with some of the "buttercream". Place the middle section on top and, likewise, spread with jam and buttercream. Add the final layer and cover the cake completely with the remaining buttercream, setting some aside for the final decoration.

5 Sprinkle praline all over the ring cake, pressing some of the praline carefully into the sides. Transfer the remaining buttercream into a piping bag with a star nozzle attached and use this to pipe 12 stars on top. Decorate each star with a cherry, then chill for at least 2 hours.

TIP:
While the custard is cooling, keep stirring it to prevent a skin from forming. If a skin does develop, use a blender briefly to process it until smooth again.

GINGER BISCUIT CREAM CAKE
WITH A FRUITY NOTE

For a 24cm (9½in) springform tin (12–14 pieces)

For the base:

100g (3½oz)	vegan ginger biscuits
350g (12oz)	plain flour
200g (7oz)	fine cane sugar
2 tsp	baking powder
75ml (2½fl oz)	rapeseed oil
2–3 tsp	vanilla extract
450ml (15fl oz)	carbonated mineral water

For the filling:

600ml (1 pint)	soya cream, suitable for whipping, well chilled
100g (3½oz)	vegan ginger biscuits
2	small tins of mandarin oranges, including juice (about 450g/1lb)
20g (¾oz)	agar-agar

For the topping:

250ml	carton soya cream, suitable for whipping, well chilled
1	sachet cream stiffener
50g (1¾oz)	vegan ginger biscuits

Time: 45 mins prep + 1 hr baking

1 Preheat the oven to 160°C (325°C/Gas 2). For the base, blitz the ginger biscuits in a food processor to create fine crumbs, or bash them in a freezer bag. Combine the biscuit crumbs, flour, sugar, and baking powder in a bowl. Mix the dry ingredients with the rapeseed oil, vanilla extract, and mineral water using a large spoon until you have a smooth consistency.

2 Line a springform tin with baking paper, transfer the cake mix into the tin, and bake in the centre of the oven for about 1 hour, until an inserted skewer comes out clean. Remove from the oven, leave to cool completely, and slice in half horizontally. Place the bottom half on a cake platter and put a cake ring around it.

3 For the filling, whip the soya cream until it is stiff. Finely crumble the ginger biscuits in a freezer bag and fold the crumbs into the cream. Spread half the cream on the base and let it firm up slightly. Drain the mandarins in a sieve, catching the juice in a pan. Then bring the juice to the boil with the gelling powder, stirring constantly. Lower the temperature and leave to simmer for a further 2 minutes. Allow to cool slightly, spread the mandarins and juice over the cream layer, and cover with the remaining cream. Place the upper section of your cake on top.

4 For the topping, whip the soya cream with the cream stiffener and spread this all over the cake. There should be some cream left over. Break the ginger biscuits into rough chunks and use these along with the remaining cream to add the finishing decorative touches to the cake. Chill the cake until ready to serve.

CHESTNUT LAYER CAKE
WITH HAZELNUT NOUGAT

For a 24cm (9½in) springform tin (12 pieces)

Time: 45 mins prep + 40 mins baking + at least 3 hrs chilling

For the base:

300g (10oz)	plain flour
200g (7oz)	fine cane sugar
2 tsp	baking powder
2 tsp	bicarbonate of soda
½ tsp	salt
30g (1oz)	vegan cocoa powder
400ml (14fl oz)	soya milk
1½ tbsp	cider vinegar
150ml (5fl oz)	rapeseed oil

For the topping:

600ml (1 pint)	soya cream suitable for whipping, well chilled
1	slightly heaped tsp agar-agar
125g (4½oz)	vegan dark chocolate, roughly chopped
150g (5½oz)	chestnut purée

Also:

190g (6½oz)	hazelnut spread, vegan
150ml (5fl oz)	soya cream, suitable for whipping, well chilled
80g (2¾oz)	chestnut purée

1 Preheat the oven to 180°C (350°F/Gas 4). For the base, combine the flour, sugar, baking powder, bicarbonate of soda, and salt. Sift over the cocoa powder and fold it in. Whisk together the soya milk and cider vinegar, leave to thicken for 5 minutes, then stir in the rapeseed oil. Quickly mix the liquid and dry ingredients with a large spoon.

2 Line a springform tin with baking paper, transfer the cake mix into the tin, and bake in the centre of the oven for about 40 minutes, until an inserted skewer comes out clean. Leave to cool completely. Place the base on a cake plate and surround with a cake ring.

3 For the topping, bring 300ml (10fl oz) of the soya cream to the boil over a moderate heat with the agar-agar and the chocolate and simmer for a few minutes, stirring carefully until the chocolate melts. Leave the cream to cool slightly, remembering to stir occasionally.

4 Whip the remaining soya cream for 3 minutes using an electric whisk on its highest setting. Use a hand blender to combine the chestnut purée with the warm chocolate and cream mixture. Once the chocolate cream mixture has cooled, fold in the whipped cream and spread swiftly over the base of your cake. Smooth the surface with a spoon and chill thoroughly in the fridge for 3 hours.

5 To decorate, first melt the hazelnut spread in a bain-marie. Spread most of the melted spread over the surface of your cake, then spread the remaining spread over a board. Leave the cake and the spread to cool. Whip the cream with the chestnut purée and transfer to a piping bag with a star nozzle attached. Cut the solidified spread into pieces. Carefully release the cake from the ring, pipe on 12 generous swirls, and top each one with a square of the cooled spread.

MOUSSE AU CHOCOLAT
RASPBERRY CAKE

Uncooked but nonetheless spectacular! The biscuit base is topped with a layer of enticing chocolate mousse and jewel-like raspberries.

For a 24cm (9½in) springform tin (12 pieces)

Time: 30 mins prep + 4 hrs chilling

For the base:

225g (8oz)	vegan caramel cookies
125g (4½oz)	vegan margarine

For the filling:

400g (14oz)	vegan dark chocolate
900ml (1½ pints)	soya cream, suitable, for whipping, well chilled
2–3 tbsp	rum
175g (6oz)	raspberries, plus
12	raspberries for decoration

Also:

100ml (3½fl oz)	soya cream, suitable for whipping, well chilled

1 To make the base, blitz the biscuits in a food processor until you have fine crumbs. Melt the margarine and mix with the crumbs until well combined. Line a springform tin with baking paper and spread the biscuit mixture over the base, using a spoon to press it down firmly and smooth the surface. Chill for at least 2 hours.

2 For the topping, melt the dark chocolate in a bain-marie and leave to cool slightly. Whip the cream with an electric mixer on its highest setting for 3 minutes then add the chocolate. It is important for the cream to combine well with the chocolate. If required, use a spatula to scrape the chocolate from the base and sides of the bowl and stir it all through thoroughly. Flavour the mousse with the rum and beat everything again vigorously.

3 Spread half of the mousse over the biscuit base. Scatter the raspberries evenly over the surface and cover with the remaining mousse, smoothing the surface. Leave to chill for a few hours.

4 Whip the cream for decorating, decant into a piping bag with a nozzle of your choice attached, and pipe 12 large swirls of cream onto the cake. Put 1 raspberry on top of each swirl of cream. Chill until ready to serve.

TIP:
Soya cream whips more easily when it is extremely well chilled. Chill the cream the previous day and, if you prefer a firmer consistency, stir in 1 sachet of cream stiffener. If children are going to be eating this cake, simply leave out the rum.

This thoroughly chocolatey gateau with its dark sponge cake, delicate chocolate cream, and sublime raspberries will add a touch of extravagance to any dessert table.

DARK CHOCOLATE AND RASPBERRY GATEAU

For a 24cm (9½in) springform tin (12 pieces)

Time: 40 mins prep + 40 mins baking + at least 3 hrs chilling

For the base:

300g (10oz)	plain flour
200g (7oz)	fine cane sugar
2 tsp	baking powder
2 tsp	bicarbonate of soda
½ tsp	salt
30g (1oz)	vegan cocoa powder
400ml (14fl oz)	soya milk
1½ tbsp	cider vinegar
150ml (5fl oz)	rapeseed oil

For the filling:

450g (1lb)	vegan dark chocolate
600ml (1 pint)	soya cream, suitable for whipping, well chilled
450g (1lb)	raspberries (fresh or frozen), plus
60g (2oz)	fresh raspberries, for decorating

Also:

vegan chocolate flakes

1 Preheat the oven to 180°C (350°C/Gas 4). For the base, combine the flour, sugar, baking powder, bicarbonate of soda, and salt in a bowl. Sift over the cocoa powder and fold it in. In a separate bowl, stir the cider vinegar into the soya milk and leave to thicken for 5 minutes, then stir in the rapeseed oil with the balloon whisk. Quickly combine the liquid and dry ingredients with a large spoon.

2 Line a springform tin with baking paper, transfer the cake mix into the tin, and bake in the centre of the oven for about 40 minutes, until an inserted skewer comes out clean. Remove from the oven and leave to cool completely.

3 Meanwhile, prepare the filling. Roughly chop the dark chocolate, melt it in a bain-marie, and stir until smooth. Whip the soya cream using an electric mixer on its highest setting. Quickly beat in the chocolate until you have a homogeneous cream, then chill for 2–3 hours.

4 Slice the sponge in half and place the lower section on a cake plate, surrounded by a cake ring. Spread a thick layer of the cream mixture on top and cover with the raspberries followed by about half of the remaining cream mixture. Put the second cake layer on top and press down slightly. Cover the surface of the cake with the cream mixture, leaving some left over for the sides.

5 Remove the cake ring and spread the remaining cream over the sides of the gateau. Scatter with chocolate flakes. Distribute the remaining raspberries on top and refrigerate.

TIP:

Prepare a day in advance to let the flavours develop overnight in the fridge. Vary the fruit depending on the season; other great options include cherries (fresh or from a jar) with some kirsch drizzled over the cake.

Enjoy the vegan version of this classic recipe. Black Forest gateau is renowned for its delicate shortcrust, flavour-packed cherries, dark sponge, and delicious cream.

BLACK FOREST GATEAU

For a 24cm (9½in) springform tin (12 pieces)

Time: 45 mins prep + 65 mins baking + at least 12 hrs chilling

For the filling and decoration:

900ml (1½ pints)	soya cream, suitable whipping, well chilled
10 tbsp	cream stiffener
140ml (4¾fl oz)	kirsch
1 tbsp	ground vanilla
720g	jar of cherries
30g (1oz)	cornflour
2 tbsp	fine cane sugar
1–2 tsp	vanilla extract
12	Amarena cherries
	vegan dark chocolate flakes

For the shortcrust:

70g (2¼oz)	plain flour
80g (2¾oz)	ground hazelnuts
50g (1¾oz)	fine cane sugar
70g (2¼oz)	vegan margarine
1–2 tsp	vanilla extract

For the sponge mix:

300g (10oz)	plain flour
200g (7oz)	fine cane sugar
2 tsp	baking powder
½ tsp	salt
2 tsp	bicarbonate of soda
30g (1oz)	vegan cocoa powder
1½ tbsp	cider vinegar
400ml (14fl oz)	soya milk
150ml (5fl oz)	rapeseed oil

1 For the filling, whip the soya cream with an electric whisk on its highest setting for 2 minutes. Beat in the cream stiffener, 100ml (3½fl oz) of the kirsch, and the vanilla. Set in the fridge to chill. Preheat the oven to 180°C (350°F/Gas 4). For the shortcrust, combine the flour, hazelnuts, and sugar. Use your fingers to work in the margarine then mix in the vanilla extract. Transfer to a springform tin lined with baking paper. Smooth out the pastry and prick all over with a fork. Bake in the oven for 20–25 minutes. Leave to cool completely.

2 For the sponge mixture, combine the flour, sugar, baking powder, salt, and bicarbonate of soda. Sift in the cocoa powder. Stir the cider vinegar into the soya milk, leave to thicken for 5 minutes, then stir in the rapeseed oil. Quickly combine the liquid and dry ingredients with a large spoon. Transfer to a springform tin lined with baking paper and bake in the centre of the oven for 40 minutes. Leave to cool completely, then slice in half horizontally. Put a cake ring securely around the shortcrust base.

3 For the filling, drain the cherries but retain the juice. Mix half the juice with the cornflour, sugar, and vanilla extract. Bring the other half to the boil, remove the pan from the hob, stir in the cornflour and juice mixture, then return to the boil, while stirring. Remove from the heat again. Stir in the cherries. Once the mixture has cooled slightly, spread it over the pastry base.

4 Place one of the sponge layers on top of the cherries and press down slightly. Drizzle the sponge with 2 tablespoons kirsch, then spread one third of the cream on top. Cover with the second sponge layer, drizzle with 2 tablespoons kirsch, spread with cream, and chill briefly. Release from the cake ring and cover the sides with cream. Transfer the remaining cream to a piping bag with a star nozzle attached and pipe 12 swirls on top. Top each swirl with an Amarena cherry. Scatter chocolate flakes over top and chill overnight.

PANCAKE LAYER CAKE

A quick, gluten-free alternative to a cake or gateau. Using fresh seasonal fruit with a soft coconut cream creates a colourful and tasty treat.

Serves 12–14   **Time: 1 hr**

For the batter:

250g (9oz)	buckwheat flour
1 tsp	baking powder
½	seeds scraped from vanilla pod
2 tbsp	fine cane sugar
1	pinch of sea salt
600ml (1 pint)	cold carbonated mineral water

Also:

600ml (1 pint)	coconut cream, suitable for whipping, well chilled
400g (14oz)	strawberries
60ml (2fl oz)	rapeseed oil, for cooking
100g (3½oz)	strawberry jam coconut flakes, for decorating

1 In a large bowl, combine the buckwheat flour and baking powder. Stir in the vanilla seeds, sugar, and sea salt. Add the mineral water and mix to create a batter. Leave to stand for 20 minutes.

2 Meanwhile, whip the coconut cream and then chill it in the fridge. Trm and quarter the strawberries.

3 Heat some rapeseed oil in a pan. Add a ladle of pancake batter to the pan, spreading it out slightly. As soon as the edges have cooked firm and turned golden, flip the pancake and cook until golden on the other side. Continue in this manner until all the batter has been used.

4 Leave the pancakes to cool completely. Layer them up spreading each one with jam, whipped cream, and then toping it with strawberries. Finish with a scatter of flaked coconut over the top layer.

TIP:

Coconut cream tastes particularly delicious if you fold in a few tablespoons of toasted flaked coconut. To do this, toast the coconut flakes in a dry pan over a moderate heat until golden. Take care, as coconut flakes burn very quickly.

CHOCOLATE CAKE WITH BANANA

For a 24cm (9½in) springform tin (12–14 pieces)

Time: 40 mins prep + 12 hrs draining + 40 mins baking

For the banana cream:

1kg (2¼lb)	soya yogurt
300ml (10fl oz)	soya cream, suitable for whipping, well chilled
2 tbsp	fine cane sugar
1–2 tsp	vanilla extract
3 tbsp	cream stiffener
2	medium-sized ripe bananas

For decorating:

100g (3½oz)	soya cream, suitable for whipping, well chilled
80g (2¾oz)	vegan dark chocolate, chopped
	banana chips, roughly chopped

For the base:

300g (10oz)	plain flour
200g (7oz)	fine cane sugar
2 tsp	baking powder
2 tsp	bicarbonate of soda
½ tsp	salt
30g (1oz)	vegan cocoa powder
1½ tbsp	cider vinegar
400ml (14fl oz)	soya milk
150ml (5fl oz)	rapeseed oil

For the filling:

4	medium bananas
450ml (15fl oz)	banana juice drink
2	sachets vegan clear cake glaze

1 For the banana cream, put the soya yogurt into a sieve lined with a thick paper towel and leave to drain overnight into a bowl. For decorating, whip the cream until stiff. Melt the chocolate in a bain-marie and fold it into the cream. Refrigerate overnight.

2 To make the base, first preheat the oven to 180°C (350°F/ Gas 4). Combine the flour, sugar, baking powder, bicarbonate of soda, and salt. Sift over the cocoa powder and fold it in. Stir the cider vinegar into the soya milk, leave to thicken for 5 minutes, then stir in the rapeseed oil. Quickly stir together the liquid and dry ingredients with a spoon. Transfer to a springform tin lined with baking paper and bake for about 40 minutes. Leave to cool, transfer to a cake plate, and surround with a cake ring.

3 For the filling, peel the bananas, slice thickly, and spread them over the base. In a small pan, prepare the banana juice with the cake glaze, following the instructions on the glaze pack. As soon as it has thickened, spread the mixture over the bananas and transfer the cake to the fridge to chill.

4 For the banana cream, squeeze out the drained soya yogurt and put it into a bowl. Whip the soya cream using an electric mixer on its highest setting, then stir in the sugar, vanilla extract, and cream stiffener. Peel the bananas, mash with a fork to a fine purée, and fold this into the cream. Add the yogurt and stir everything to a smooth, firm consistency. Spread this over the glazed bananas and smooth the surface. Chill the whole cake again.

5 Transfer the chocolate cream into a piping bag with a star nozzle attached , pipe swirls around the edge of the cake and sprinkle them with banana chips. Carefully release the cake ring with the help of a sharp knife and chill the cake until ready to serve.

CHOCOLATE TART

RAW & GLUTEN-FREE

For a 28cm (11in) tart tin (12 pieces)

For the base:

100g (3½oz)	whole blanched almonds
300g (10oz)	dates, pitted
150g (5½oz)	walnuts
2 tbsp	vegan cocoa powder

For the chocolate cream:

2	avocados (Hass variety)
2	very ripe bananas
7	dates, pitted
5 tbsp	vegan cocoa powder
1 tsp	orange juice, freshly squeezed

Also:

40g (1¼oz)	fine coconut flakes, for sprinkling

Time: 20 mins prep + 1 day soaking + 2 hrs chilling

1 For the base, soak the almonds in plenty of water the day before. Leave the almonds to drain well then chop roughly in a food processor. Add all the ingredients for the base and process everything until you have a homogeneous mixture. Sprinkle the tart tin with coconut flakes. Transfer the almond mixture into the tart tin, spreading it out to 1–2cm (½–¾in) thick and creating a slight rim around the edge. Leave it to chill in the fridge.

2 For the chocolate cream, halve the avocados, remove the stones, and use a tablespoon to scoop out the flesh. Add to a food processor. Peel the bananas and roughly break into pieces. Add the bananas, dates, cocoa powder, and orange juice to the avocados and process everything to a smooth and creamy consistency. Spread this over the base and smooth the surface. Before serving, chill the tart for about 2 hours in the fridge or, if you're short of time, about 1 hour in the freezer.

COCONUT TART
WITH CHOCOLATE

This delicious gluten-free tart is simple to prepare and it tastes absolutely heavenly, so it will be popular with everyone, not just fans of coconut and chocolate.

For a 24cm (9½in) tart tin (12 pieces)

For the base:

100g (3½oz)	coconut oil
280g (9½oz)	coconut flakes
200ml (7fl oz)	agave syrup

For the filling:

300g (10oz)	vegan dark chocolate
225g (8oz)	coconut milk

Also:

vegan margarine, for greasing the tin

flaked coconut

soya cream, suitable for whipping, well chilled (optional)

Time: 25 mins prep + 15 mins baking + chilling time

1 Preheat the oven to 180°C (350°F/Gas 4). For the base, melt the coconut oil in a small pan over a low heat then set aside. Use a spoon to stir the coconut flakes and agave syrup together in a bowl. Knead in the slightly cooled coconut oil with your fingers.

2 Grease a tart tin with margarine. Transfer your mixture to a tin, creating a thick rim about 3cm (1½in) high. Smooth the base with a spoon, pressing everything down firmly. Bake in the centre of the oven for about 15 minutes, until the sides and base are pale brown – but not too dark. Remove from the oven and leave to cool slightly until the base is firm.

3 For the filling, roughly chop the dark chocolate. Bring the coconut milk to the boil in a pan over a moderate heat and stir in the chocolate, until you have a smooth consistency and there are no more lumps. Pour the chocolate cream into the base and chill the tart in the fridge for several hours, until set.

4 Toast the flaked coconut in a dry pan and scatter over the tart. Whip the soya cream, if using, with an electric mixer on its highest setting. Use the cream to decorate the tart. Serve well chilled.

TIP:

This tart is made without any flour and also contains very little sugar. Dark chocolate with a cocoa content of at least 70% is ideal for this recipe.

This splendid tart is incredibly versatile! The base can be combined with any fruit for a delicious treat; whether you use apples and pears or a thick layer of berries – this is a tart for all seasons.

WHOLEMEAL TART
WITH SEASONAL FRUIT

For a 24cm (9½in) tart tin (12 pieces)

Time: 30 mins prep + 30 mins chilling + 45 mins baking

For the base:

250g (9oz)	wholemeal spelt flour, plus extra for dusting
80g (2¾oz)	fine cane sugar
1 tsp	vanilla powder
1 tsp	baking powder
1	pinch of salt
1	grated zest of small organic lemon
1 tbsp	ground linseed
100g (3½oz)	vegan margarine, plus extra for greasing the tin

For the crumble:

150g (5½oz)	wholemeal spelt flour
100g (3½oz)	fine cane sugar
1 tsp	vanilla powder
125g (4½oz)	vegan margarine

For the filling:

60g (2oz)	ground almonds
500g (1lb 2oz)	seasonal fruit, washed and chopped

Also:

icing sugar, for dusting

1 For the base, combine the flour, cane sugar, vanilla, baking powder, salt, and lemon zest in a bowl. Stir the linseed together with 3 tablespoons of water and leave to swell for 5 minutes. Add little blobs of margarine to the flour mixture and use your fingers to rub it in, then add the linseed to create a smooth pastry mixture. Grease a tart tin and dust with flour. Transfer your pastry into the tin, pressing it out to cover the bottom and create a rim around the edge, and prick all over with a fork. Chill the pastry for at least 30 minutes.

2 Preheat the oven to 180°C (350°C/Gas 4). Meanwhile, for the crumble, combine the flour, cane sugar, and vanilla in a bowl and carefully rub in the margarine. Use your fingers to create rough crumble pieces.

3 For the filling, spread the almonds over the base and cover with the fruit. Top with the crumble and bake the tart in the centre of the oven for 35–45 minutes. Remove, leave to cool, and dust with icing sugar.

TIP:
This tart tastes delicious with a custard layer. Prepare a custard made from 350ml (12fl oz) soya milk, 3 tbsp cane sugar, 2–3 tsp vanilla extract, and 40g (1¼oz) cornflour. Spread the custard over the base of the tart instead of the almonds then add the fruit layer on top. Scatter over the crumble and bake as described.

FILLING FOOD AND SNACKS

From pizza to quiche to rolls: delicious, hearty, meat-free food, tasty party snacks and nibbles, and nutritious breads for baking enthusiasts

HAWAIIAN PIZZA

For a 30 x 40cm (12 x 15½in) baking tray

Time: 20 mins prep + 55 mins proving + 25 mins baking

For the dough:

½	cube fresh yeast
350g (12oz)	spelt flour with a high gluten content, plus extra for dusting
1 tsp	salt
1	pinch of fine cane sugar
2 tbsp	olive oil

For the sauce:

400g (14oz)	passata
100g (3½oz)	tomato purée
1 tbsp	olive oil
1 tsp	sea salt
½ tsp	ground white pepper
1	pinch of fine cane sugar
1	squeeze lemon juice
1 tsp	dried oregano

For the topping:

125g (4½oz)	smoked tofu or vegan ham
8	pineapple slices
	oregano leaves, for scattering

For the "cheese":

5 tbsp	cashew nut butter
2 tsp	yeast flakes
½ tsp	salt
¼ tsp	ground white pepper
1	squeeze lemon juice

1 To make the dough, put 200ml (7fl oz) lukewarm water into a bowl and crumble in the yeast. Cover and leave at room temperature for about 10 minutes, then use a balloon whisk to mix to a smooth consistency.

2 In a separate large bowl, combine the spelt flour, salt, and sugar. Add the olive oil and the yeast and water mixture and knead everything until you have a smooth dough. Cover and leave to prove for about 45 minutes, until doubled in size.

3 Meanwhile, for the sauce, stir together the passata, tomato purée, and olive oil. Season to taste with the sea salt, pepper, sugar, lemon juice, and oregano.

4 For the topping, roughly dice the tofu or ham. For the "cheese", stir 3 tablespoons of water into the cashew nut butter. Add the yeast flakes, salt, pepper, and lemon juice to taste.

5 Preheat the oven to 200°C (400°C/Gas 6) and line a baking tray with baking paper. Knead the dough vigorously once more and roll it out on a work surface dusted with flour until it is the size of the baking tray. Spread the tomato sauce, topping, and then the "cheese" over the dough. Bake the pizza in the centre of the oven for 20–25 minutes until golden brown. Remove, slice into 12 portions, and scatter with oregano leaves before serving.

TIP:
This pizza also tastes delicious with pickled tofu, strips of pepper and onion, cherry tomatoes, mushrooms, or pumpkin.

TARTE FLAMBÉE

With a crisp, thin base topped with delicious pointed cabbage, this vegan tarte flambée is just as good as the original!

For a 30 x 40cm (12 x 15½in) baking tray

Time: 15 mins prep + 2 hrs proving + 25 mins baking

For the dough:

250g (9oz)	plain flour
½ tsp	salt
1	pinch of fine cane sugar
100ml (3½fl oz)	mild-tasting soya drink
2 tbsp	olive oil

For the topping:

300g (10oz)	pointed cabbage
3	onions
1	carrot
200g (7oz)	smoked tofu or smoked tempeh
2 tbsp	rapeseed oil
1 tsp	salt
½ tsp	freshly ground white pepper
1	pinch of grated nutmeg
½ tsp	caraway

Also:

200g (7oz)	vegan crème fraîche
20g (¾oz)	pine nuts

1 To make the dough, combine the flour, salt, and sugar in a bowl. Add the soya drink and olive oil and knead everything vigorously until you have a homogeneous, soft dough. Cover and leave the dough to prove in a warm place for at least 2 hours.

2 Meanwhile, for the topping, halve the pointed cabbage, cut out the stalk in a V-shaped wedge, and slice the cabbage into roughly 1cm (½in) wide strips. Peel the onions and carrots, cut in half, and slice into thin strips. Dice the smoked tofu.

3 Heat the rapeseed oil in a large non-stick pan over a high heat and sear the tofu until it is nice and crisp. Reduce the heat and add the pointed cabbage, carrots, and onions. Cook over a moderate heat, stirring frequently, being sure not to let the vegetables colour too much. Season with the salt, pepper, nutmeg, and caraway.

4 Preheat the oven to 200°C (400°F/Gas 6). Knead the dough vigorously again, divide into two portions, and roll these out as thinly as possible. Lay the pieces on a baking tray lined with baking paper and cover with a thin layer of crème fraîche. Spread the topping out evenly then drizzle over the remaining crème fraîche. Bake the tarte flambée in the centre of the oven for 20–25 minutes, until slightly crisp and golden brown. Scatter the pine nuts over the tart about 10 minutes before the end of the baking time. Remove from the oven and enjoy while still warm.

The combination of savoy cabbage, lentils, and tomatoes on a yeast dough is quite simply brilliant. You've just got to give it a try!

SAVOY CABBAGE TART

For a 30 x 40cm (12 x 15½in) baking tray

Time: 45 mins prep + 55 mins proving + 35 mins baking

For the dough:

½	cube fresh yeast
350g (12oz)	spelt flour with a high gluten content
1 tsp	salt
1	pinch of fine cane sugar
2 tbsp	olive oil

For the topping:

85g (3oz)	dried brown lentils
400g (14oz)	savoy cabbage
2	onions
2	garlic cloves
100g (3½oz)	tomato purée
3½ tbsp	red wine or vegetable stock
500g	can chopped tomatoes
1	pinch of herbal salt and freshly ground black pepper
½ tsp	sweet paprika
1	pinch of grated nutmeg
½	juice of lemon

Also:

3½ tbsp	olive oil, for frying

1 To make the dough, crumble the yeast into a bowl containing 200ml (7fl oz) lukewarm water. Cover and leave to prove in a warm place for about 10 minutes, then whisk until smooth with a balloon whisk. Combine the flour, salt, and sugar in a large bowl. Add the olive oil and the water and yeast mixture and work until you have a smooth dough. Cover and leave to prove in a warm place for 30–45 minute, until doubled in size.

2 Meanwhile, for the topping, cook the lentils according to the packet instructions, strain off the water, and leave to drain. Remove the stalk from the savoy cabbage and slice into diamonds. Peel and finely dice the onions and garlic. Heat the olive oil in a large pan, add the savoy cabbage, and sauté over a high heat. Add the onions, garlic, and tomato purée and cook briefly. Quickly deglaze with red wine and add the tomatoes. Season to taste with the herbal salt, pepper, paprika, nutmeg, and lemon juice. Finally, fold in the lentils.

3 Preheat the oven to 200°C (400°F/Gas 6) and line a baking tray with baking paper. Knead the dough again vigorously and roll it out on the baking tray. Spread the savoy cabbage and lentil mixture on top and bake in the centre of the oven for 30–35 minutes. Remove and enjoy while still warm.

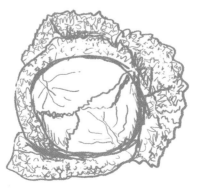

ONION TART

This tart is easy to make, filling, and tastes fabulous!

For a 30 x 40cm (12 x 15½in) baking tray

Time: 20 mins prep + 1 hr proving + 45 mins baking

For the dough:

½	cube fresh yeast
350g (12oz)	spelt flour with a high gluten content, plus extra for dusting
2 tbsp	olive oil
1 tsp	salt
1	pinch of fine cane sugar

For the filling:

8	onions
1	garlic clove
1	long leek
1–2	red peppers
4 tbsp	vegan margarine
200ml (7fl oz)	vegetable stock
300g (10oz)	oat cream, well chilled
5 tsp	almond butter
8 tbsp	yeast flakes
1 tbsp	caraway
1 tsp	salt and freshly ground black pepper

1 To make the dough, put 200ml (7fl oz) lukewarm water into a large bowl, crumble in the yeast, and use a balloon whisk to dissolve it in the water. Add the flour, olive oil, salt, and sugar and knead everything until you have a homogeneous dough. If the dough is too sticky, add a bit more flour. Wrap the dough in cling film and put it in the fridge for at least 1 hour.

2 For the topping, peel the onions and garlic. Slice the leek and onions into very fine rings, mince the garlic and dice the peppers. In a high-sided pan, melt the margarine over a moderate heat and sauté the leek, onions, and garlic. Add the diced pepper, dust with flour, and continue to sauté briefly. Gradually add the vegetable stock, oat cream, and almond butter and thicken slightly, stirring constantly. Season to taste with the yeast flakes, caraway, and salt and pepper.

3 Preheat the oven to 200°C (400°F/Gas 6). Line a baking tray with baking paper and roll out the dough on it. Prick the dough with a fork, then top with the leek and onion mixture. Bake the onion tart in the centre of the oven for 40–45 minutes until golden; it is ready if the crust sounds hollow when tapped. Remove and enjoy while still warm.

TIP:

If you really feel this dish could do with some "bacon", replace the peppers with 200g (7oz) chopped mushrooms, drizzle with 2 tbsp olive oil and soy sauce, and season with pepper. Spread on the tart before baking.

127

QUICHE LORRAINE

For a 24cm (9½in) springform tin (12–14 pieces)

Time: 30 mins prep + 1 hr chilling + 35 mins baking

For the pastry:

300g (10oz)	plain flour, plus extra for dusting
1 tsp	salt
150g (5½oz)	vegan margarine

For the filling:

150g (5½oz)	smoked tofu
1	garlic clove
10	spring onions
250g (9oz)	soya cream
150g (5½oz)	vegan cheese, grated
1 tsp	salt
½ tsp	freshly ground black pepper
½ tsp	ground turmeric
1	pinch of grated nutmeg

Also:

3 tbsp	rapeseed oil, for frying

1 For the pastry, combine the flour with the salt. Add the margarine in little blobs and work it in with your fingers. Gradually add 8 tablespoons water and combine everything until you have a smooth shortcrust. Wrap in cling film and put in the fridge for about 1 hour.

2 Roll out the pastry on a surface dusted with flour and transfer it into a springform tin lined with baking paper, or a well-greased quiche tin dusted with flour. Shape the pastry to create a 5cm (2in) high edge, press it down firmly, and prick with a fork. Put the tin in the fridge to chill while you prepare the filling.

3 Cut the smoked tofu into little cubes and finely chop the garlic. Slice the spring onions into thin rings. Heat the oil over a high heat in a non-stick pan and briefly sear the tofu cubes. Then reduce to a moderate heat and sauté the cubes until brown on all sides. Add the spring onions and finally the garlic and continue to cook briefly. Tip the contents of the pan onto a large plate lined with kitchen paper and let the excess fat drain away.

4 Preheat the oven to 180°C (350°F/Gas 4). In a large bowl, combine the soya cream with the cheese and season with the salt, pepper, turmeric, and nutmeg. Fold in the tofu mixture and spread everything over the quiche base, smoothing the surface. Bake in the centre of the oven for 30–35 minutes. Remove and enjoy while still warm.

TIP:

Instead of shop-bought vegan cheese you can also use the cashew nut "cheese" from the Hawaiian pizza (see p.120).

Macadamia nuts introduce a bit of bite and, along with the slightly astringent rocket, they combine beautifully with the delicate spinach and tomato filling.

SPINACH QUICHE

For a 28cm (11in) springform tin (12–14 pieces)

Time: 20 mins prep + 1 hr chilling + 1 hr baking

For the pastry:

325g (11oz)	spelt flour with a high gluten content
150g (5½oz)	vegan margarine, plus extra for greasing the tin
1 tsp	salt
1	pinch of cane sugar

For the filling:

20g (¾oz)	vegan margarine
450g (1lb)	spinach leaves (frozen)
1	onion
1	garlic clove
200g (7oz)	cherry tomatoes
300g (10oz)	spelt cream (available online)
100g (3½oz)	vegan cheese, grated
1 tsp	salt
½ tsp	freshly ground black pepper
1	pinch of freshly grated nutmeg
25g (scant 1oz)	macadamia nuts

Also:

100g (3½oz)	rocket
2 tbsp	olive oil, to drizzle

1 To make the pastry, combine the flour, margarine, salt, sugar, and 8 tablespoons of water in a bowl until it forms a dough. Wrap the pastry in cling film and chill in the fridge for 1 hour. Grease a springform tin, roll out the pastry, and place it in the tin. Shape the pastry so that the sides come up to create a border.

2 Preheat the oven to 200°C (400°F/Gas 6). For the filling, melt the margarine in a large high-sided pan. Add the spinach and sauté over a low heat. Peel the onion and garlic, dice finely, and add to the spinach. Halve the cherry tomatoes and add these, too. Pour in the cream and add the vegan cheese.

3 Season the filling to taste with salt, pepper, and the nutmeg and pour it into the pastry case. Bake the quiche in the centre of the oven for 50–60 minutes until golden. Chop the macadamias and scatter over the quiche about 10 minutes before the end of the cooking time. Remove the quiche and release from the tin to serve, scatter with the rocket, and drizzle with olive oil.

"Pide", a type of Turkish flatbread, is a delicious alternative to pizza and is just as versatile as its Italian relative when it comes to toppings. The main difference is the shape.

PIDES

Makes 2 pides

Time: 25 mins prep + 45 mins proving + 15 mins baking

For the dough:

250g (9oz)	plain flour
½	sachet dried yeast
1	pinch of fine cane sugar
1 tsp	salt

For the topping:

200g (7oz)	spinach leaves (frozen)
200g (7oz)	broccoli florets (frozen)
100g (3½oz)	peas (frozen)
1	pinch of salt
1	small onion
1	small red pepper
125g (4½oz)	oat cream
	freshly ground black pepper, to taste
2 tbsp	pine nuts

Also:

3½ tbsp	soya milk
50g (1¾oz)	sesame seeds

1 To make the dough, combine the flour with the yeast, sugar, and salt in a bowl. Add 150ml (5fl oz) water and knead into a smooth dough. Cover and leave to prove in a warm place for 30–45 minutes, until doubled in size.

2 Preheat the oven to 200°C (400°F/Gas 6) and line a baking tray with baking paper. Halve the dough and roll out each piece on the baking tray until they are about a finger-width thick. The dough should be oval, with the ends tapering to a point.

3 For the topping, briefly blanch the spinach, broccoli, and peas in slightly salted boiling water, then drain. Peel the onion and slice into thin rings, then deseed the pepper and chop it into cubes. Spread both pides with the oat cream and top with the vegetables, seasoning to taste. Scatter with the pine nuts, then gently fold up the edges of the dough. Brush the edges of the pides with some soya milk, scatter with the sesame seeds, and bake in the centre of the oven for 15 minutes. Remove and enjoy while still warm.

Savoury muffins are a great snack, and also a fabulous dish to tak to a celebration or garden party. The delicious spelt flour with smo tofu offers something quite new in terms of flavour.

SPICED MUFFINS

Makes 12 muffins

100g (3½oz)	smoked tofu
1	red onion
3 tbsp	rapeseed oil, for frying
200g (7oz)	spelt flour
1 tsp	baking powder
1 tsp	salt
½ tsp	freshly ground black pepper
1 tsp	sweet paprika
150g (5½oz)	vegan margarine
3½ tbsp	unsweetened soya milk

Time: 25 mins prep + 25 mins baking

1 Finely dice the tofu and the red onion. Heat the rapeseed oil over a moderate heat in a non-stick pan. Sauté the tofu and onion.

2 Preheat the oven to 180°C (350°F/Gas 4). Put paper cases into the moulds of a muffin tray. In a large bowl, combine the flour with the baking powder and the spices. Add the margarine in little blobs and rub it in with your fingers. Gradually incorporate the soya milk followed by the onion and tofu mixture.

3 Transfer the mixture into the muffin cases and bake in the centre of the oven for 20–25 minutes, until an inserted skewer comes out clean. Remove from the oven. You can eat the muffins warm or cold.

TIP:

Instead of smoked tofu, you could also dice 100g (3½oz) sweet potato, marinade it in soy sauce, and sauté with the onions. For a really wonderful smoky aroma, try using smoked paprika.

Ready in a flash, these herby straws will be gobbled up instantly by party guests!

PARTY STRAWS

Makes 30 straws

Time: 20 mins prep + 20 mins baking

For the party straws:

5	ready-made puff pastry sheets (15 × 15cm/6 x 6in each); see pp.14 and 15, chilled
40g (1¼oz)	vegan cheese, grated
1 heaped tsp	caraway
1 heaped tsp	coarse sea salt
1 heaped tsp	dried rosemary

Also:

3½ tbsp	soya milk, for brushing

1 Cut each puff pastry sheet into 6 equal-sized strips. Brush each of the 30 strips with soya milk. Scatter equal quantities of cheese and caraway over half of the pastry strips and scatter the other half with sea salt and rosemary.

2 Preheat the oven to 180°C (350°C/Gas 4). Twist the pastry strips and place them on a baking tray lined with baking paper. Bake in the centre of the oven for 15–20 minutes, until golden. Remove and eat when they are lukewarm or cold.

TIP:

It's important to work quickly with the puff pastry and while it is still cold. You can also make a sweet version of these party straws by sprinkling them with cinnamon sugar.

CIABATTA ROLLS

Makes 8–10 rolls

20g (¾oz)	fresh yeast
300g (10oz)	plain flour, plus extra for dusting
2 tbsp	olive oil
1 tsp	salt
½ tsp	fine cane sugar
3½ tbsp	soya milk, for brushing (optional)

Time: 10 mins prep + 65 mins proving + 20 mins baking

1 Pour 150ml (5fl oz) lukewarm water into a large bowl. Crumble in the yeast, cover, and leave in a warm place to rest for about 10 minutes. Combine with a balloon whisk, then add the flour, olive oil, salt, and sugar and knead until it forms a supple dough. Cover and leave to prove in a warm place for 30–45 minutes, until doubled in size.

2 Preheat the oven to 200°C (400°F/Gas 6). On a floured work surface, shape the dough into a long log and roll this out until it is about a finger-width thick. To make the ciabatta rolls, cut this sheet into 8–10 equal-sized rectangles, cover, and leave to prove for a further 20 minutes.

3 Either dust the ciabatta rolls with flour or, if you prefer a smooth surface, brush with soya milk. Bake the rolls in the centre of the oven for 15–20 minutes. Remove and leave to cool slightly.

When you need a recipe that is both quick to make and healthy, these Kamut® rolls are just perfect. Kamut® is a nutrient-rich, ancient variety of wheat, which is once again being cultivated today.

SPEEDY WHOLEGRAIN ROLLS

Makes 20 rolls

Time: 10 mins prep + 10 mins proving + 25 mins baking

For the dough:

1	cube fresh yeast
750g (1lb 10oz)	Kamut®, freshly milled, or wholewheat flour
1 tsp	sea salt
½ tsp	ground allspice
1 tsp	ground turmeric

Also:

3½ tbsp	soya milk, for brushing
	pumpkin seeds, poppy seeds, or sesame seeds, for sprinkling (optional)

1 Crumble the yeast into a bowl containing 500ml (16fl oz) lukewarm water, cover, and leave in a warm place for 10 minutes. Combine the flour, sea salt, allspice, and turmeric in a separate bowl. Whisk the yeast and water and add to the flour mixture. Knead everything until it forms a smooth dough.

2 Preheat the oven to 200°C (400°F/Gas 6) and line a baking tray with baking paper. Form around 20 equal-sized rolls from the dough, place them on the baking tray, brush with soya milk, and sprinkle with the seeds of your choice, if using. Bake the rolls in the centre of the oven for about 25 minutes. Remove and leave to cool slightly.

TIP:
If you spray the rolls with water halfway through the baking time, this makes the crust nice and crunchy. These rolls are perfect for freezing.

PUMPKIN AND BUCKWHEAT ROLLS

Makes 12 rolls

500g (1lb 2oz)	buckwheat flour
1 tsp	cream of tartar
2 tbsp	guar gum
1 tsp	sea salt
½ tsp	ground allspice
1	pinch of ground aniseed
3½ tbsp	linseed oil
500ml (16fl oz)	carbonated mineral water
100g (3½oz)	pumpkin seeds

Time: 10 mins prep + 30 mins baking

1 In a large bowl, combine the flour with the cream of tartar, guar gum, sea salt, allspice, and aniseed. Add the linseed oil and mineral water and work everything together until it forms a smooth dough. Knead in the pumpkin seeds.

2 Preheat the oven to 200°C (400°F/Gas 6) and line a baking tray with baking paper. Divide the dough into 12 equal-sized portions and shape these into oval rolls. Place the rolls on the baking tray and make several diagonal incisions in the surface of each one. Bake the rolls in the centre of the oven for about 30 minutes. Remove and leave to cool slightly. These rolls are also perfect for freezing.

TIP:

Take care when shopping to buy baking powder that is explicitly labelled as gluten-free. Some baking powders continue to include tiny amounts of wheat flour. Gluten-free products are often labelled with a crossed out ear of wheat.

Muesli to go: this recipe takes your favourite muesli and transforms it into an easy to transport bread roll. Ideal for when you're on the move.

MUESLI ROLLS

Makes 6 rolls

400g (14oz)	wholemeal spelt flour
150g (5½oz)	muesli of your choice
¾ tsp	salt
250ml (9fl oz)	almond milk, plus extra for brushing
1½ tbsp	agave syrup
1	cube fresh yeast
30g (1oz)	vegan margarine

Time: 20 mins prep + 85 mins proving + 30 mins baking

1 Combine the flour, muesli, and salt in a large bowl. Warm the almond milk over a low heat and pour it into a separate bowl. Stir in the agave syrup, crumble in the yeast, and stir everything gently. Cover and leave in a warm place for about 10 minutes.

2 Melt the margarine in a pan and add to the flour and muesli mixture. Stir the almond milk and yeast mixture once again then add this to the dough mixture. Knead everything thoroughly to form a smooth, pliable dough – if necessary add a bit more almond milk. Cover and leave the dough to prove in a warm place for 45 minutes, until doubled in size.

3 Shape 6 rolls from the dough, make a cross incision in the top of each one, and leave to prove for a further 30 minutes.

4 Preheat the oven to 200°C (400°F/Gas 6). Brush the rolls with some almond milk and bake in the centre of the oven for 20–30 minutes. Remove from the oven and leave to cool slightly.

SESAME BAGELS

Makes 10 bagels

400g (14oz)	strong plain flour, plus extra for dusting
1 tsp	salt
25g (scant 1oz)	vegan margarine
1	cube fresh yeast
1 tsp	fine cane sugar
3½ tbsp	soya milk, for brushing
3 tbsp	pale sesame seeds

Time: 25 mins prep + 85 mins proving + 15 mins baking

1 Add the flour and salt to a large bowl and create a well in the centre. Warm the margarine with 250ml (9fl oz) water in a small pan over a low heat until it has melted. Leave the mixture to cool a little until it's lukewarm. Crumble in the yeast and add the sugar. Cover the mixture and leave to stand for about 10 minutes, then combine with a balloon whisk and pour into the well in the centre of the flour. Knead everything until it forms a smooth dough. Shape the dough into a ball, cover, and leave to prove in a warm place for about 45 minutes, until doubled in size.

2 Dust your work surface with flour. Divide the dough as evenly as possible into 10 pieces and shape these into balls. Use the handle of a wooden spoon to make a hole in the centre of each ball to create a ring. Use your fingers to widen the hole in each dough ring to about 2–3cm (¾–1½in).

3 Line a baking tray with baking paper and place the bagels on it. Leave to prove for another 30 minutes. Brush the tops of the bagels with soya milk and scatter evenly with sesame seeds. Set the oven to 230°C (450°F/Gas 8); do not preheat. Put the bagels into the centre of the cold oven and bake for about 15 minutes. Remove and leave to cool on a wire rack.

TIP:

If you make bagels regularly, you can buy a special tool that lets you quickly mould the bagels so they are all the same size and shape.

This potato bread is soft and moist, and tastes equally great with sweet or savoury toppings. It also stays fresh for several days.

SOFT POTATO BREAD

Makes 1 medium-sized loaf

Time: 40 mins prep + 2¼ hrs proving + 30 mins baking

For the yeast starter mix:

150ml (5fl oz)	soya milk
2 heaped tsp	bread spices (see below)
50g (1¾oz)	spelt flour
1	sachet dried yeast
1 tbsp	agave syrup

For the main dough:

100ml (3½fl oz)	soya milk
3 tbsp	soya yogurt
1	squeeze lemon juice
400g (14oz)	spelt flour, plus extra for dusting
1½ tsp	salt
300g (10oz)	potatoes, peeled and cooked

1 To make the starter mix, warm the soya milk in a pan with the bread spices and then set aside. Combine the flour and dried yeast in a bowl. Stir the agave syrup into the spiced soya milk then mix everything into the dry ingredients until well combined. Cover and leave to prove in a warm place for about 15 minutes, then stir until smooth again.

2 For the main dough, whisk together the soya milk, soya yogurt, and lemon juice then warm over a low heat. Remove from the heat. Combine the flour and salt in a bowl. Mash the potatoes and add them to the flour. Stir in the soya milk, yogurt, and lemon juice mixture. Then add the starter mix and knead everything until you have a smooth dough, possibly adding a bit of soya milk or flour, if required. Cover and leave to prove in a warm place for about 1 hour, until doubled in size.

3 Knead the dough vigorously and shape it into an oval loaf. Place this on a baking tray lined with baking paper, dust with flour, and leave to prove again for about 1 hour. Preheat the oven to 200°C (400°F/Gas 6). Make 4 incisions in the top of the loaf and bake in the centre of the oven for 30 minutes. If the bread begins to darken too quickly, cover it with foil. Remove and leave to cool.

TIP:

If the bread sounds hollow when you tap on the base, it is ready. You can make your own delicious bread spice by finely grinding fennel, coriander, caraway, cardamom, aniseed, and blue fenugreek in a pestle and mortar.

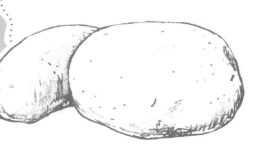

Packed with nutrients, full of flavour, and super quick to bake, this tasty bread is ideal for those with a gluten intolerance.

PUMPKIN AND AMARANTH BREAD

For a 28cm (11in) long loaf tin

Time: 25 minutes prep + 35 minutes baking

300g (10oz)	buckwheat flour, plus extra for dusting
70g (2¼oz)	puffed amaranth
100g (3½oz)	ground sesame seeds
1 tsp	baking powder
½ tsp	sea salt
1 tsp	ground turmeric
2 tsp	guar gum
2 tbsp	olive oil
500ml (16fl oz)	carbonated mineral water
100g (3½oz)	pumpkin seeds
	vegan margarine, for greasing the tin

1 Combine the flour with the amaranth, sesame seeds, baking powder, sea salt, turmeric, and guar gum in a bowl. Add the olive oil and mineral water and knead everything swiftly to form a smooth dough. Work in the pumpkin seeds.

2 Preheat the oven to 200°C (400°F/Gas 6). Transfer the dough to a greased loaf tin dusted with flour and bake in the centre of the oven for 30–35 minutes, until an inserted skewer comes out clean. Remove and leave to cool completely in the tin before turning out the loaf.

TIP:

If you can't find ground sesame seeds, you can also use the whole seeds. If so, reduce the quantity of liquid slightly or adjust the amount of flour accordingly.

This delicious bread is a huge hit thanks to the nutritious spelt, the vitamin-rich carrots, and the healthy fats in the walnuts.

CARROT AND WALNUT BREAD

For a 32cm (13in) long loaf tin (2 loaves)

Time: 30 mins prep + 70 mins proving + 45 mins baking

380ml (13fl oz)	soya milk, plus extra for brushing
1	cube fresh yeast
100g (3½oz)	walnuts
50g (1¾oz)	vegan margarine, plus extra for greasing the tin
500g (1lb 2oz)	carrots
2 tbsp	lemon juice
750g (1lb 10oz)	spelt flour with a high gluten content, plus extra for dusting
½ tsp	salt
1	pinch of fine cane sugar

1 Gently heat the soya milk in a small pan over a low heat. Pour into a bowl, crumble in the yeast, cover, and leave at room temperature for about 10 minutes. Then stir until smooth with a balloon whisk.

2 Roughly chop the walnuts and toast them in a dry pan. Add the margarine and let it melt. Peel and finely grate the carrots, then mix them with the lemon juice in a bowl.

3 In a large bowl, combine the flour, salt, and sugar. Work in the milk and yeast mixture, then add the walnut and margarine mix plus the grated carrot. Knead everything until it forms a smooth and supple dough. Shape it into a ball, cover, and leave to prove in a warm place for about 40 minutes, until doubled in size.

4 Knead the dough vigorously once more and shape into 2 small loaves. Put these into a well-oiled loaf tin dusted with flour. Cover and leave for a further 20 minutes. Preheat the oven to 190°C (375°F/Gas 5). Make diamond-shaped incisions in the top of the bread and brush the top with a bit of soya milk. Bake in the centre of the oven for 40–45 minutes. Remove and leave to cool slightly.

TIP:
Fill a small, heat-resistant bowl with water and put it in the oven during baking – this will make the bread even more moist.

WINTRY AND CHRISTMASSY

Delicious treats for festive months: fill your veggie kitchen with holiday fragrances and introduce a bit of winter magic. Rustle up sensational recipes packed with nostalgia and guaranteed to delight young and old alike.

APPLE STRUDEL

Makes 1 strudel (10–12 portions)

Time: 35 mins prep + 30 mins resting + 35 mins baking

For the pastry:

300g (10oz)	plain flour, plus extra for dusting
1	pinch of salt
2 tbsp	rapeseed oil
20g (¾oz)	vegan margarine, for brushing

For the filling:

1.5kg (3lb 3oz)	apples (such as Bramley)
110g (3¾oz)	vegan margarine
50g (1¾oz)	breadcrumbs
1	juice and grated zest, organic lemon
50g (1¾oz)	raisins
2 tbsp	rum
50g (1¾oz)	ground almonds
80g (2¾oz)	fine cane sugar
1 tsp	ground cinnamon
	salt

Also:

icing sugar, for dusting

1 Boil some water in a pan. To make the pastry, sift the flour into a pile on the work surface and create a well in the centre. Add the salt, rapeseed oil, and 120ml (4fl oz) lukewarm water to the well and use your hands to combine everything to a smooth consistency. Don't overwork the ingredients, otherwise the pastry will become tough and be liable to tear. Shape it into a ball, brush with margarine, and transfer to a plate. Pour away the boiled water, and leave the pastry to rest for 30 minutes under the upturned warm pan.

2 Meanwhile, for the filling, peel and core the apples, divide into 8 sections, then slice into 5mm (¼in) thick crescents. Melt half the margarine in a pan and cook the breadcrumbs until they are pale brown. Mix the apples with the lemon juice and zest, the raisins, rum, almonds, sugar, cinnamon, and salt.

3 Preheat the oven to 200°C (400°F/Gas 6). Melt the remaining margarine and set aside. Press the ball of strudel pastry flat on a tea towel dusted with flour, then roll it out with a rolling pin. Lift up the pastry with both hands and stretch it out over the backs of your hands until it is paper thin and measures around 60 × 60cm (24 x 24in).

4 Brush about half the margarine in a thin layer over the pastry. Spread the breadcrumbs over the lower quarter of the pastry sheet, leaving a gap of 3cm (1½in) around the edge. Put the filling on top of the crumbs. Fold the outer edges of the pastry over the filling. Roll up the strudel, using the towel to help you and place it with the seam edge facing down on a baking tray lined with baking paper. Use a brush to carefully remove any excess flour.

5 Brush the rest of the melted margarine over the strudel and bake on the middle shelf of the oven for 30–35 minutes. Remove, leave to cool briefly, and serve while it is still warm. Dust generously with icing sugar before serving.

TIP:

Warm strudel goes beautifully with cold vanilla ice cream or a delicious vanilla sauce (see p.189).

This simple strudel is perfect for when you need to rustle up something quickly, but without compromising on taste. It will even win over your granny.

SPEEDY POPPY SEED STRUDEL
WITH RUM RAISINS

Makes 1 strudel (10–12 portions)

Time: 10 mins prep + 25 mins baking

For the strudel:

1	ready-made roll puff pastry (250g/9oz); see pp.14 and 15
250g (9oz)	ground poppy seeds
150g (5½oz)	fine cane sugar
25g (scant 1oz)	breadcrumbs
5 tbsp	rum
4–6 tbsp	soya milk, plus extra for brushing
50g (1¾oz)	raisins, soaked overnight in rum

Also:

icing sugar, for dusting

1 Remove the puff pastry from the fridge 10 minutes in advance. Combine the ground poppy seeds with the cane sugar and breadcrumbs in a bowl. Pour in the rum, then gradually stir in just enough soya milk to create a spreadable paste. This can vary depending on how finely ground the poppy seeds are.

2 Lay the puff pastry on the work surface and spread the poppy seed mixture evenly over it, leaving a gap of 3cm (1½in) all around the edge. Scatter the rum-soaked raisins over the poppy seed filling.

3 Preheat the oven to 180°C (350°F/Gas 4). Roll up the strudel from the long edge then fold in the ends, pressing them together slightly. Lift carefully onto a baking tray with the seam facing down and brush with soya milk. Bake the strudel in the centre of the oven for about 25 minutes. Remove and dust with icing sugar. Leave to cool completely.

TIP:

To make an almond strudel, replace the poppy seeds with ground almonds and the soya milk with almond milk. Simply leave out the rum and raisins.

CHRISTMAS STOLLEN

Makes 1 large Christmas stollen (15–20 slices)

Time: 25 mins prep + 55 mins proving + 70 mins baking

For the stollen mix:

600g (1lb 5oz)	plain flour
75g (2½oz)	ground almonds
100g (3½oz)	fine cane sugar
2 heaped tbsp	soya flour
1	pinch of salt
250ml (9fl oz)	soya milk
1–2 tsp	vanilla extract
1	cube fresh yeast
1 tsp	rum
50g (1¾oz)	candied lemon peel
50g (1¾oz)	candied orange peel
125g (4½oz)	soft vegan margarine
100g (3½oz)	raisins
100g (3½oz)	marzipan

Also:

3 tbsp	vegan margarine
250g (9oz)	icing sugar

1 Combine the flour, almonds, cane sugar, soya flour, and salt in a large bowl. Heat the soya milk in a pan over a low heat, add the vanilla extract, then pour it into a separate bowl. Crumble in the yeast, cover, and leave to prove in a warm place for 10 minutes. Then stir until smooth with a spoon and add to the dry ingredients along with the rum, candied lemon peel, candied orange peel, margarine, raisins, and marzipan. Knead everything until well combined, cover, and leave to prove in a warm place for 45 minutes.

2 Preheat the oven to 180°C (350°F/Gas 4). Line a baking tray with a double layer of baking paper to prevent the stollen from becoming too dark on the bottom. Create a loaf shape from the dough using both hands, making a shallow depression lengthways down the centre. Bake the stollen in the centre of the oven for 60–70 minutes, turning it halfway through the baking time, until an inserted skewer comes out clean. Leave to cool completely on a wire rack.

3 To create the icing sugar coating, melt the margarine over a low heat and brush the stollen all over with it. First, dust the base of the stollen liberally with icing sugar, then do the same on the top. The stollen tastes best if left for a week to allow the flavours to develop.

TIP:

Instead of working marzipan into the dough, you can give the stollen a marzipan filling. Roll 200g (7oz) marzipan into a log shape and place it in the centre of the stollen during the shaping process. Proceed as described in the recipe.

PUMPKIN STOLLEN

For a 30cm (12in) long loaf tin

100g (3½oz)	raisins
	rum
300g (10oz)	Hokkaido pumpkin, or small red squash
130ml (4½fl oz)	soya milk
500g (1lb 2oz)	plain flour, plus extra for your hands
180g (6¼oz)	fine cane sugar
1	sachet dried yeast
	grated zest of
1	organic lemon
1 tsp	vanilla powder
½ tsp	ground ginger
½ tsp	ground allspice
1	pinch of salt
100g (3½oz)	vegan margarine, plus extra for greasing the tin

Time: 12 hrs soaking + 30 mins prep + 75 mins proving + 1 hr baking

1 Soak the raisins overnight in rum. Dice the pumpkin and cook it in a pan with the soya milk over a moderate heat until soft. Process it to a purée with a hand blender and leave to cool slightly. In a large bowl, combine the flour, sugar, dried yeast, lemon zest, vanilla, ginger, allspice, and salt.

2 Melt the margarine in a small pan and stir it into the pumpkin purée. Use floured hands to work the purée into the dry ingredients, kneading everything to create a supple dough. Incorporate the rum-raisins and, depending on how moist or dry the dough is, add some extra soya milk or flour, as required. Cover and leave to prove for about 45 minutes in a warm place.

3 Preheat the oven to 180°C (350°F/Gas 4). Knead the dough once again. Grease a large loaf tin, put the dough inside, and leave to prove for about another 30 minutes. Bake the stollen in the centre of the oven for about 1 hour. If the stollen begins to go too brown, cover it with foil. Remove and leave it to cool completely.

TIP:

You can leave the skin of the Hokkaido pumpkin on as it tastes really delicious. Eat the stollen plain, dusted with icing sugar, or spread with vegan margarine.

163

Different German regions have different names for these traditional dough figures, including "Weckmann", "Stutenkerl", and "Krampus". Whichever name, they are usually baked and eaten around the time of Saint Nicholas' Day in Germany.

"WECKMÄNNER" DOUGH FIGURES

Makes 6 dough figures

Time: 25 mins prep + 70 mins proving + 20 mins baking

For the dough:

350ml (12fl oz)	soya milk
1	cube fresh yeast
675g (1½lb)	plain flour
1½ tsp	salt
100g (3½oz)	fine cane sugar
100g (3½oz)	soft vegan margarine
1–2 tsp	vanilla extract

Also:

raisins, to decorate

soya milk, for brushing

1 To make the dough, warm the soya milk over a low heat and remove from the heat. Crumble in the yeast, cover, and leave to stand at room temperature for 10 minutes. Combine the flour with the salt and sugar in a bowl. Add the margarine in little blobs and work it in slightly with your fingers until the lumps are no longer visible. Add the vanilla extract. Make a well in this mixture and pour in the milk and yeast mixture. Slowly work the ingredients together to form a supple dough. Knead the dough for 5 minutes, cover, and leave to prove in a warm place for 30 minutes, until it has doubled in size. Then knead it once again.

2 Line a baking tray with baking paper and shape little dough figures from the mixture. To do this, split the dough into 6 equal portions, roll each piece into a fairly thick sausage shape, and flatten it slightly. Snip the top of the dough at the sides slightly and round it off to make the head. To make the legs, make a vertical incision at the bottom and pull the two sections apart. Make the arms in a similar manner.

3 Lay the little figures on a baking tray, press in raisins for the eyes, mouth, and buttons, and brush the dough with soya milk. Cover and leave to prove in a warm place for about 30 minutes. Meanwhile, preheat the oven to 200°C (400°F/Gas 6). Bake in the centre of the oven for 15–20 minutes. Remove and leave to cool completely.

TIP:

To make your dough figures a consistent size and shape, it helps to create a paper template to guide you when shaping the dough.

This traditional spiced loaf is wonderfully moist and nutty, with Christmassy flavours that smell delicious before it's even cook

MUM'S SPICE BREAD

Makes 4 small 25cm (10in) loaves

750g (1lb 10oz)	apples
200g (7oz)	walnuts
500g (1lb 2oz)	raisins
2 tbsp	rum
1 tbsp	vegan cocoa powder
250g (9oz)	fine cane sugar
500g (1lb 2oz)	plain flour
½ tsp	baking powder
¾ tsp	salt
1½ tsp	ground cloves
1½ tsp	ground cinnamon
1½ tsp	ground allspice
2 tbsp	ground linseed

Time: 35 mins prep + 12 hrs steeping + 90 mins baking

1 One day ahead, grate the apples, including the skin, into a bowl. Add the walnuts, raisins, rum, cocoa powder, and sugar and combine everything thoroughly. Cover the bowl with cling film and leave to steep overnight in the fridge.

2 The following day, add the flour, baking powder, salt, and spices. Stir 3 tablespoons of water into the linseed, leave to swell for a few minutes, then add this to the mix. Knead everything until you have a smooth dough. The dough is very heavy, so it's important to knead in the flour vigorously with your hands to prevent lumps forming.

3 Preheat the oven to 180°C (350°F/Gas 4). Transfer the dough into 4 25cm (1in) loaf tins and bake in the centre of the oven for 80–90 minutes. If the bread starts to go too brown, cover the surface with baking paper. Remove the loaves and leave to cool completely.

TIP:

This spice bread tastes even more sophisticated if you combine two or three types of apple. If stored in a cool place, it will keep for several weeks and it can also be frozen very successfully.

CHOCOLATE BISCUIT CAKE

For a 28cm (11in) long loaf tin

250g (9oz)	coconut oil
240g (8½oz)	icing sugar
100g (3½oz)	vegan cocoa powder
1 tsp	vanilla extract
50	vegan plain biscuits
100g (3½oz)	white vegan chocolate (optional)

Time: 30 mins prep + at least 2–3 hrs chilling time

1 Melt the coconut oil in a small pan over a low heat. Combine the icing sugar and cocoa powder and add these to the coconut oil in the pan. Add the vanilla extract and use a balloon whisk to mix these ingredients into the coconut oil.

2 Line a loaf tin with cling film and put in a thin layer of the chocolate mixture, smoothing the surface. Top with a layer of biscuits, followed by a layer of chocolate mixture, and continue in this manner until all the biscuits and mixture have been used. The final layer should be a chocolate layer smoothed out to create a nice even finish.

3 Put the chocolate biscuit cake into the fridge to chill for at least 2–3 hours, until it is completely firm. Turn it out onto a board or flat plate and pull off the cling film. If using, melt the white chocolate in a bain-marie and spoon over the cake to decorate. Return the chocolate biscuit cake to the fridge until ready to serve.

"LEBKUCHEN" COOKIES

Makes 50 cookies

Time: 20 mins prep + 30 mins resting + 15 mins baking

For the dough:

500g (1lb 2oz)	strong wholemeal flour, plus extra for dusting
225g (8oz)	fine cane sugar
4 tbsp	vegan cocoa powder
2 tbsp	mixed spices (cinnamon, ground cloves, allspice, ginger, mace, and ground cardamom)
1 tsp	baking powder
250ml (9fl oz)	soya cream
3 tbsp	rapeseed oil
2–3 tsp	vanilla extract
1 tbsp	amaretto

For the glaze:

125g (4½oz)	icing sugar
½ tsp	orange juice
50	whole blanched almonds

Also:

soya milk, for brushing

1 To make the dough, combine the flour, cane sugar, cocoa powder, spices, and baking powder in a bowl. In a separate bowl, combine the soya cream, rapeseed oil, vanilla extract, and amaretto, then add these to the dry ingredients. Knead everything until you have a supple dough, adding a bit more liquid if required, then leave to rest for about 30 minutes.

2 Preheat the oven to 180°C (350°F/Gas 4). Roll out the dough to about 1cm (½in) thick on a work surface dusted with flour and stamp out stars, hearts, and other shapes. Place these on a baking tray lined with baking paper and brush with soya milk. Bake the cookies in batches in the centre of the oven for 12–15 minutes. Remove and leave to cool completely.

3 Make a thick glaze by stirring together icing sugar, 2 tablespoons of water, and the orange juice. Brush this over the cookies. Put one almond on each cookie and leave to dry on a wire rack. Store in a biscuit tin.

TIP:
You can also use lemon juice to make the icing sugar glaze, and the almonds can be replaced with hazelnuts.

CHRISTMAS BISCUITS

Makes 35–40 cookies

Time: 35 mins prep + 30 mins chilling + 15 mins baking

For the dough:

2 tbsp	chickpea flour
300g (10oz)	wholemeal flour, plus extra for dusting
75g (2½oz)	fine cane sugar
1 tsp	baking powder
½	juice of lemon
1–2 tsp	vanilla extract
2	drops bitter almond oil
200g (7oz)	vegan margarine

Also:

3 tbsp	soya milk
250g (9oz)	strawberry jam
1 tbsp	icing sugar, plus extra for dusting (optional)

1 Stir the chickpea flour together with 2 tablespoons of water until smooth. In a large bowl, combine the wholemeal flour, cane sugar, and baking powder. Add the chickpea flour paste, lemon juice, vanilla extract, and almond oil. Then add the margarine in blobs and knead everything until it forms a supple dough. Wrap in cling film and leave to rest in the fridge for at least 30 minutes.

2 Dust the work surface with flour and roll the dough out thinly. Use circular or Christmas biscuit cutters to stamp out shapes. In half of these shapes, use a smaller cutter to stamp out a design in the centre, making sure you leave a border of about 5mm (¼in). Keep re-rolling any remaining dough and stamping until the dough has all been used. You should have equal numbers of solid bases and tops with patterns cut in them.

3 Preheat the oven to 200°C (400°F/Gas 6). Line a baking tray with baking paper, place the biscuits on it, and brush the tops with soya milk. Bake the biscuits in the centre of the oven for 12–15 minutes. Remove and leave to cool completely.

4 Press the jam through a sieve into a small pan. Bring the jam to the boil briefly over a low heat. Remove from the heat and then use a spoon to spread it over the biscuit bases. If desired, dust the cut out biscuit tops with icing sugar before setting them on the bases. Leave to dry.

MUESLI COOKIES

Makes 30–35 biscuits

Time: 20 mins prep + 20 mins baking

200g (7oz)	strong wholemeal flour
50g (1¾oz)	fine cane sugar
1 tsp	ground cinnamon
1	pinch of ground allspice
1	pinch of ground aniseed
90ml (3fl oz)	rapeseed oil
100ml (3½fl oz)	almond milk
1–2 tsp	vanilla extract
200g (7oz)	muesli of your choice

1 Preheat the oven to 180°C (350°F/Gas 4). In a large bowl, combine the flour, sugar, cinnamon, allspice, and aniseed. Stir together the rapeseed oil and almond milk and add the vanilla extract. Add these to the dry ingredients and mix until you have a smooth consistency. Carefully fold in the muesli.

2 Line a baking tray with baking paper. Use 2 tablespoons to scoop out the mixture into roughly 3cm (1½in) large dollops on the baking tray, pressing each one down slightly. Bake the biscuits in the centre of the oven for 15–20 minutes. Remove and leave to cool completely on a wire rack.

TIP:

A fan oven is not suitable for this recipe as the cookies can easily become too dry and the dried fruit in the muesli is liable to burn.

Vanilla crescents are a great addition to the festive season – there should be some in every cookie jar. It's important to make them with real vanilla, as that is what gives them their fabulous flavour.

VANILLA CRESCENTS

Makes 30–35 crescents

Time: 25 mins prep + 1 hr chilling + 20 mins baking

For the dough:

300g (10oz)	plain flour
100g (3½oz)	fine cane sugar
90g (3¼oz)	ground almonds
1–2	seeds scraped from vanilla pods
1	splash of lemon juice and some lemon zest
200g (7oz)	vegan margarine, chilled

Also:

60g (2oz)	icing sugar
1 tsp	vanilla powder

1 In a large bowl, combine the flour, cane sugar, almonds, and vanilla seeds. Add the lemon juice and zest, then add the margarine in little blobs. Work everything together swiftly with your fingers until you have a supple, well-combined dough. Wrap in cling film and leave in the fridge for about 1 hour.

2 Preheat the oven to 190°C (375°F/Gas 5) and line a baking tray with baking paper. Shape little rolls from the dough, bend and taper them into crescent shapes, and lay them on the baking tray. Bake the crescents in the centre of the oven for 15–20 minutes. Remove them from the oven, leave to cool briefly, then dust them with a combination of icing sugar and ground vanilla while they are still warm.

TIP:

The scraped out vanilla pod can be used to make delicious vanilla sugar. Just fill a preserving jar with fine sugar and add the vanilla pod. After 7 days the sugar will have absorbed the flavour.

Spiced cookies are a traditional German recipe made using shortcrust. In the past, wooden moulds were used to stamp Christian motifs on the biscuits. Nowadays you will find all sorts of other decorative patterns, too.

SPICED COOKIES

Makes about 30 cookies

Time: 35 mins prep + 1 hr chilling + 15 mins baking

1 tbsp	chickpea flour
250g (9oz)	plain flour
1 tsp	baking powder
80g (2¾oz)	fine cane sugar
1	pinch of ground cardamom
1	pinch of ground cloves
½ tsp	ground cinnamon
100g (3½oz)	vegan margarine
1–2 tsp	vanilla extract
50g (1¾oz)	ground almonds

1 Stir the chickpea flour with 2 tablespoons of water until smooth. Sift the plain flour into a large bowl. Add the baking powder, sugar, and spices and mix everything together thoroughly. Add the chickpea flour paste, the margarine in little blobs, and the vanilla extract. Using the dough hook on an electric mixer, combine everything into a smooth dough, gradually adding the almonds. Wrap the dough in cling film and chill in the fridge for at least 1 hour (see below).

2 Preheat the oven to 180°C (350°F/Gas 4). Roll the dough out thinly and stamp out shapes with a cookie cutter. Place the little cookies on a baking tray lined with baking paper and bake in the centre of the oven for 10–15 minutes. Remove them from the oven and leave to cool completely.

TIP:
These spiced cookies taste even better if you prepare the dough the previous evening and leave it to chill overnight.

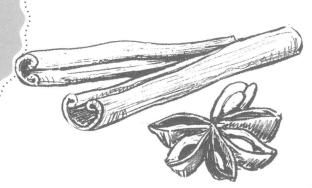

These shortbread biscuits are usually made with lots of eggs, but it's not hard to make a vegan version. Most of the ingredients will already be in your store cupboard.

PIPED SPIRALS
WITH RASPBERRY JAM

Makes 8 spirals

225g (8oz)	soft vegan margarine
110g (3¾oz)	icing sugar, well sifted
½ tsp	vanilla powder
1	pinch of salt
250g (9oz)	spelt flour
50g (1¾oz)	cornflour
1	jar good-quality raspberry jam (about 350g/12oz)
250g (9oz)	vegan dark chocolate

Prep: 40 mins + 15 mins baking time

1 Preheat the oven to 180°C (350°F/Gas 4). Cream the margarine and icing sugar in a bowl with an electric whisk on its highest setting until light and fluffy. Stir in the vanilla powder and salt. Combine the spelt flour and cornflour, then stir these in, too.

2 Transfer the mixture to a piping bag with a star nozzle attached. Line a baking tray with baking paper and pipe 16 spiral rings. Bake in the centre of the oven for about 15 minutes, until the biscuits just turn slightly golden, but are not too dark. Remove and leave to cool completely.

3 In a small pan, warm the jam over a low heat. Remove from the heat and spread a generous quantity of jam over half of the biscuit rings. Place the remaining halves on top and leave to set. Melt the dark chocolate in a bain-marie. Dip the rings into the chocolate to decorate as desired, then leave to dry on a wire rack. Store in a tin in a cool, dry location.

TIP:
The dough may vary in consistency depending on the flour. If it is too firm, a bit of soya cream can be added to make it softer. If it is too soft, some extra flour will make it stiffer. These spiral biscuits are also delicious with a vegan chocolate and hazelnut spread.

NUT WEDGES

Makes 8–10 nut wedges

Time: 25 mins prep + 30 mins baking + 30 mins cooling

For the base:

300g (10oz)	plain flour
100g (3½oz)	fine cane sugar
2 tsp	soya flour
2 tsp	baking powder
175g (6oz)	vegan margarine
2–3 tsp	vanilla extract

For the topping:

200g (7oz)	soft vegan margarine
200g (7oz)	fine cane sugar
2–3 tsp	vanilla extract
100g (3½oz)	chopped hazelnuts
300g (10oz)	ground hazelnuts

Also:

4 tbsp	apricot jam
200g (7oz)	vegan dark chocolate

1 To make the base, combine the flour, sugar, soya flour, and baking powder in a large bowl. Add the margarine in little blobs, then add the vanilla extract and quickly knead everything to a smooth consistency. Roll out the dough onto a baking tray lined with baking paper. Bring the apricot jam to the boil with 2–3 tablespoons of water in a small pan over a low heat, stir until smooth, and brush this over the base.

2 Preheat the oven to 180°C (350°F/Gas 4). For the topping, combine the margarine with the sugar, vanilla extract, and the chopped and ground hazelnuts, until it forms a coherent mixture. Spread this evenly over the base and smooth the surface.

3 Bake in the centre of the oven for 25–30 minutes. Remove the baking tray from the oven and leave to cool for about 30 minutes. Slice into ten 10cm (4in) squares then divide these in half diagonally to create triangles.

4 Chop the dark chocolate into pieces and melt in a bain-marie. Dip the tips of the nut wedges into the chocolate and leave on a wire rack to dry.

TIP:

Nut wedges taste great with any kind of nut, for instance, a mixture of walnuts, hazelnuts, and almonds. The combination of ground and chopped nuts gives the biscuits their crunchy bite.

FRUIT PUNCH CUBES

Makes 15 cubes (depending on size)

Time: 35 mins prep + 55 mins baking

For the cake mixture:

675g (1½lb)	plain flour
300g (10oz)	fine cane sugar
1 tsp	baking powder
	zest of
1	organic lemon
350ml (12fl oz)	rapeseed oil
2–3 tsp	vanilla extract
450ml (15fl oz)	carbonated mineral water
	vegan margarine, for greasing the baking tray

For the filling:

125g (4½oz)	vegan dark chocolate, plus extra for decorating
12 tbsp	apricot jam
6 tbsp	fine cane sugar
1	splash of rum

For the glaze:

300g (10oz)	icing sugar
6 tbsp	red wine
4 tbsp	rum

1 Preheat the oven to 200°C (400°F/Gas 6). To make the cake mixture, combine the flour, cane sugar, and baking powder in a bowl. Add the lemon zest, rapeseed oil, and vanilla extract. Stir in the mineral water with a spoon and combine everything swiftly to a smooth consistency – it doesn't matter if there are a couple of little lumps remaining. Spread the mixture over a greased baking tray and bake in the centre of the oven for about 15 minutes. Then lower the temperature to 150°C (300°F/Gas 2) and continue to bake for an additional 40 minutes, until the cake is golden brown and an inserted skewer comes out clean. Remove from the oven and leave to cool completely.

2 To make the filling, melt the dark chocolate in a bain-marie. Crumble one third of the cake into a bowl and combine with the apricot jam, sugar, rum, and chocolate until you have a firm consistency. Slice the remaining cake in half crossways. Spread the chocolate and fruit mixture over the lower section, replace the top section, and press down firmly. Use a sharp knife to slice the cake into little cubes.

3 For the glaze, stir the icing sugar into the red wine and rum until smooth, then dunk the little cake cubes into the glaze. If you wish, grate some dark chocolate on top.

TIP:

The consistency of the glaze should not be too thin, so add the liquid gradually to the icing sugar and stir until smooth. You can also briefly freeze the cubes before glazing, spike them with a fork, dunk in the glaze, then leave to dry and in the fridge. The cubes can be glazed twice, if desired.

BASIC RECIPES

YEAST DOUGH For a 30 x 40cm (12 x 15½in) baking tray
Prep: 20 mins + 55 mins proving time + baking time

½ cube fresh yeast | 350g (12oz) spelt flour with a high gluten content | 1 tsp salt | pinch of fine cane sugar | 2 tbsp olive oil

Pour 200ml (7fl oz) lukewarm water into a bowl and crumble in the yeast. Cover and leave to ferment in a warm place for 10 minutes. Meanwhile, combine the flour, salt, sugar, and olive oil. Whisk the yeast and water mixture, add to the other ingredients, and knead everything until you have a supple dough. Cover and leave to prove in a warm place for about 45 minutes, until doubled in size. Knead it once again, roll out the dough, place it on the baking tray, and proceed as described in your recipe.

SWEET YEAST DOUGH

For a 30 x 40cm (12 x 15½in) baking tray
Prep: 20 mins + 55 mins proving time + baking time

500g (1lb 2oz) strong wheat flour | 3 tbsp fine cane sugar | ¼ tsp salt | 100ml (3½fl oz) soya milk, plus about 8 tbsp lukewarm soya milk | 1–2 tsp vanilla extract | ½ cube fresh yeast | zest of ¼ organic lemon | 80g (2¾oz) soft vegan margarine

Sift the flour into a large bowl. Add the sugar and salt and combine. Create a well in the centre. Gently heat 100ml (3½fl oz) soya milk in a small pan, then pour it into the well. Add the vanilla extract. Crumble the yeast into the milk, then cover the mixture and leave to stand in a warm place for about 10 minutes. Stir this yeast mix into the dry ingredients, add the lemon zest and margarine in little blobs, and knead everything until you have a smooth

dough. Depending on how the dough turns out, you may need to add more lukewarm soya milk or flour, the result should be a soft, but not sticky, dough. Cover the dough and leave to prove for 45 minutes, until it has doubled in size. Knead vigorously once again, then proceed as described in your recipe.

PUFF PASTRY For a 30 × 40cm (12 x 15½in) baking tray
Prep: 1 hr + about 1½ hrs chilling time

550g (1¼lb) plain flour, plus some more for dusting | 5g salt | pinch of fine cane sugar | 500g (1lb 2oz) vegan margarine

To make the basic pastry, combine 500g (1lb 2oz) flour, the salt, sugar, 50g (1¾oz) margarine, and 300ml (10fl oz) water, and knead until smooth with the dough hook of an electric mixer. Wrap in cling film and chill for 30 minutes. For the margarine layer, quickly knead 450g (1lb) margarine into 50g (1¾oz) flour, making sure your hands are cold, and shape into an 18 × 18cm (7 x 7in) slab. Wrap in cling film and chill for 30 minutes. Roll out the basic pastry on a floured work surface to create a 1cm (½in) thick slab. Place the margarine layer on top of this slab of pastry. Fold the corners of the pastry in like an envelope towards the centre, enclosing the fat layer inside as you do so and pressing the edges firmly together. Roll it out to a size of approximately 60 × 20cm (24 x 8in) and 1cm (½in) thick. Fold one-third of the pastry towards the centre, then fold a third of the pastry over this from the other side. Gently press the slab of pastry flat with the rolling pin, first crossways then lengthways. Chill for about 20 minutes. Roll out the pastry again to create a 60 x 20cm (24 x 8in) slab. Fold the two narrow sides in to the centre, then fold once again to get 4 layers. Roll it out and repeat the initial fold-roll operation. Chill the pastry for 20 minutes. Then repeat the second fold-roll operation. Chill for 30 minutes and roll out to create 10 slabs of pastry, each roughly 5mm thick and 15 x 15cm (6 x 6in). If well wrapped, these will keep in the fridge for about 7 days.

TIP:
To make pizza, try putting the dough in the fridge for 24 hours to rise slowly, which results in a particularly light texture.

SHORTCRUST PASTRY For a 28cm (11in) springform tin
Prep: 20 mins + 1 hr chilling time + baking time

300g (10oz) plain flour | 1 tsp salt | 150g (5½oz) vegan margarine

In a large bowl, combine the flour with the salt and add the margarine in little blobs. Work the ingredients together with 8 tbsp water until you have a smooth pastry. Wrap in cling film and chill for 1 hour. Line the springform tin with baking paper. Roll out the pastry and lay it in the tin; if required, pull the edges up the sides to create a rim. Follow the instructions in your recipe for working with the pastry.

SIMPLE CAKE MIX For a 28cm (11in) springform tin
Prep: 10 mins + 40 mins baking time

300g (10oz) plain flour | 2 tbsp cornflour | 125g (4½oz) fine cane sugar | 15g (½oz) baking powder | pinch of salt | 120ml (4fl oz) rapeseed oil | 140ml (4¾fl oz) soya milk | 2–3 tsp vanilla extract | 150ml (5fl oz) carbonated mineral water

Preheat the oven to 180°C (350°C/Gas 4). In a large bowl, combine the flour, cornflour, sugar, baking powder, and salt. Stir the rapeseed oil into the soya milk until smooth, add the vanilla extract, and mix into the dry ingredients. Add the mineral water and swiftly stir all the ingredients with a large spoon until you have a smooth consistency. Follow your recipe, adding any spices required. Transfer the mixture to your tin and bake for about 40 minutes. Proceed as described in the recipe, maybe topping with some fruit.

PALE SPONGE MIX For a 30 × 40cm (12 x 15½in) tray or a 28cm (11in) springform tin
Prep: 10 mins + 50 mins baking time

450g (1lb) plain flour | 240g (8½oz) fine cane sugar | 15g (½oz) baking powder | some zest from 1 organic lemon | 1 tsp ground vanilla | 2 tbsp cornflour | 100ml (3½fl oz) rice milk | 100ml (3½fl oz) corn oil | 350ml (12fl oz) carbonated mineral water

Preheat the oven to 180°C (350°C/Gas 4). In a large bowl, combine the flour, sugar, baking powder, lemon zest, vanilla, and cornflour. Mix the rice milk and corn oil and stir into the dry ingredients. Finally, carefully fold in the mineral water with a large spoon. Spread the mixture over the tray or transfer it into the tin and bake for about 50 minutes.

DARK SPONGE MIX For a 30 × 40cm (12 x 15½in) tray or a 28cm (11in) springform tin
Prep: 10 mins + 40 mins baking time

300g (10oz) plain flour | 200g (7oz) fine cane sugar | 30g (1oz) vegan cocoa powder | 2 tsp baking powder | 2 tsp bicarbonate of soda | ½ tsp salt | 400ml (14fl oz) soya milk | 1½ tbsp cider vinegar | 150ml (5fl oz) rapeseed oil

Preheat the oven to 180°C (350°C/Gas 4). In a large bowl, combine the flour, sugar, cocoa powder, baking powder, bicarbonate of soda, and salt. In a separate bowl, whisk the cider vinegar into the soya milk and leave to thicken for about 5 minutes. Then stir in the rapeseed oil until smooth. Swiftly combine the dry and liquid ingredients with a large spoon. Spread the mixture over the tray or transfer it into the tin and bake for about 40 minutes.

BATTER For 1 portion
Prep: 15 mins

350g (12oz) wholemeal flour | 1 sachet baking powder | 1 tbsp olive oil | 250ml (9fl oz) beer or other carbonated liquid | 1 tsp salt | fine cane sugar | ½ portion vegan whipped "egg whites" (see p.188 for the recipe)

Combine the flour and baking powder in a large bowl. First add the olive oil, then the beer (or other liquid) and stir everything swiftly with a large spoon until smooth. Add the salt and sugar. Carefully fold in the vegan whipped egg white. Proceed as described in the recipe. For example, for apple fritters, dip the apple rings in the batter, fry in plenty of fat, and leave to drain on kitchen paper.

MERINGUES **For 8–15 meringues (depending on size)**
Prep: 30 mins + 2 hs baking time

1 portion vegan whipped "egg whites" (200ml/7fl oz, see recipe, right) | 125g (4½oz) icing sugar | 1 tsp guar gum | 1 tsp vanilla extract

Preheat the oven to 130°C (250°F/Gas ½). Follow the recipe for vegan "egg whites", right. Sift the icing sugar into a bowl, add the guar gum and vanilla sugar and mix. Fold the mixture spoon by spoon into the egg whites and beat using an electric whisk on its highest setting. Transfer to a piping bag with a star nozzle and pipe equal-sized blobs onto a baking tray lined with baking paper. Let the meringues dry out in the centre of the oven for 1½–2 hours. Remove the meringues and leave to cool completely. Store in an airtight container.

COOKIE DOUGH **For 25–30 cookies**
Prep: 35 mins + 1 hr chilling time + 15 mins baking time

300g (10oz) strong wheat flour, plus some more for dusting | 90g (3¼oz) fine cane sugar | 1 tsp chickpea flour | 1–2 tsp vanilla extract | 200g (7oz) vegan margarine | 125g (4½oz) icing sugar | juice of ½ lemon | colourful sugar strands, to decorate

In a large bowl, combine the flour and cane sugar. Stir 2 tsp water into the chickpea flour to create a paste, add the vanilla extract, then add to the dry ingredients. Add blobs of margarine and combine everything quickly to make a smooth mixture. Wrap the dough in cling film and chill for about 1 hour. Preheat the oven to 180°C (350°F/Gas 4). Generously dust a work surface with flour (or line it with baking paper), roll out the cookie dough, and stamp out shapes. Place these on a baking tray lined with baking paper. Bake in the centre of the oven for 10–15 minutes. Remove and leave to cool completely. To make the icing, sift the icing sugar into a bowl. Stir in a teaspoon of lemon juice at a time, stirring it into the icing sugar until smooth. The aim is to create a thick glaze. Spread it over the biscuits and decorate with sprinkles.

LINSEED "EGG WHITES" **For 1 portion**
Prep: 5 mins + 30 mins cooking time + 1 hr chilling time

40g (1¼oz) linseed

Bring the linseed and 500ml (16fl oz) water to the boil in a pan. Simmer over a low heat for 20–25 minutes, until it forms a gel-like consistency. Strain the contents of the pan into a bowl through a fine sieve to separate the gel from the linseed granules. Chill the gel for 1 hour, then beat it for several minutes with an electric whisk or a food processor on its highest setting to create a neutral-tasting plant-based foam.

GLACÉ ICING **For 1 round cake (24cm/9½in springform) or 1 loaf cake (26cm/10½in long tin)**
Prep: 5 mins

125g (4½oz) icing sugar | 2–3 tbsp lemon juice, water, or some other liquid (juice, syrup, milk, tea, liqueur, coffee, red wine, rum) | nuts, grated chocolate, colourful sugar strands, to decorate (optional)

Sift the icing sugar into a bowl and add the liquid a few drops at a time – the quantity will depend on the desired consistency of your icing. Stir with the balloon whisk until you have a smooth, very viscous mixture. For icing with a stronger flavour and which is more "opaque", add less liquid. Apply the icing as soon as possible because it sets quickly. Using hot liquid to make the icing helps it bind successfully and gives it a particularly wonderful sheen after it has dried. If you want to add any decorations, this needs to be done soon after the icing has been applied.

TIP:
It's easy to make your own piping bag for decorating: just cut out a triangle of baking paper, roll it up into a cone (with the point sealed), and fold over the top edge. Fill it half full of melted chocolate, snip off the tip, and decorate your baked goods in whatever style you like.

FROSTING For 1 round cake (24cm/9½in springform) or 1 loaf cake (26cm/10½in long tin) or 12 cupcakes
Prep: 15 mins

200g (7oz) soft vegan margarine | about 400g (14oz) icing sugar | about 4 tbsp juice, jam, or fruit compote, as desired and at room temperature

Cream the margarine in a bowl until light and fluffy, then sift in the icing sugar and combine. Add teaspoonful's of the juice, jam, fruit compote, or other flavouring, stirring carefully. The quantity can vary depending on the desired consistency – very runny ingredients need more icing sugar; more viscous and cohesive ingredients, such as fruit purées, need less. Spread the cake with the frosting.

APRICOT GLAZE For 1 round cake (24cm/9½in springform tin) or 1 loaf cake (26cm/10½in long tin)
Prep: 10 mins

4 tbsp apricot jam | 1 tbsp orange juice

Purée the jam and press it through a fine sieve. Stir it into the orange juice in a pan and simmer for about 2 minutes over a low heat. Spread the hot glaze over your cake with a pastry brush and leave to dry. Using an apricot glaze gives cakes, tarts, and other baked items a great flavour and keeps them fresh for longer. The icing on creamy gateaux stays in place better if you use an apricot glaze.

VANILLA CUSTARD For about 500g (1lb 2oz) custard
Prep: 15 mins

500ml (16fl oz) soya, rice, or oat milk | 40g (1¼oz) cornflour | 2–3 tsp vanilla extract

Stir the cornflour and a little milk until smooth. Put the remaining milk into a pan and bring to the boil with the vanilla extract over a moderate heat. Remove from the heat and stir in the cornflour paste with a whisk. Bring it back to the boil, stirring constantly, until you have a thick custard – the longer it cooks, the thicker it will become.

VANILLA SAUCE For about 600ml (1 pint) sauce
Prep: 15 mins

500ml (16fl oz) almond milk | 2 heaped tbsp cornflour | seeds from 1 vanilla pod, plus the pod itself | 3 tbsp fine cane sugar | pinch of salt | 200g (7oz) coconut cream

Take 4 tbsp of the almond milk and stir in the cornflour with a whisk until smooth. Put the remaining milk into a pan and bring to the boil over a moderate heat. Add the vanilla seeds, vanilla pod, sugar, salt, and coconut cream and return to the boil, stirring constantly. Remove from the heat and quickly stir in the cornflour paste with a whisk. Continue to cook until the sauce has thickened. Warm vanilla sauce goes well with strudel and other dishes.

BUTTERCREAM TOPPING
For 1 round cake (24cm/9½in springform)
Prep: 15 mins

350g (12oz) vanilla custard (see left, cooked until thick) | 200g (7oz) soft vegan margarine | 80g (2¾oz) icing sugar

Allow the thick, cooked custard to cool to room temperature. Meanwhile, cream the margarine in a bowl, sift over the icing sugar, and stir it in. Carefully stir the custard into the margarine and icing sugar mixture. Spread a thick layer over your cake and leave to chill.

CREAM TOPPING For 1 round cake (24cm/9½in springform) or 1 loaf cake (26cm/10½in long tin) Prep: 10 mins

1 pack soya cream, suitable for whipping (300g/10oz), well chilled | 1 sachet cream stiffener | extra ingredients to add flavour and/or colour as desired (vanilla extract, cinnamon, vegan food colouring, etc.)

Whip the soya cream using an electric whisk on its highest setting for at least 3 minutes, sprinkling in the cream stiffener as you do so. Beat in any additional ingredients. Use the topping to add the finishing touches to a cake then leave the cake to cool completely.

INDEX

THE AUTHORS ...

Jérôme Eckmeier has worked at numerous prestigious restaurants both in Germany and abroad since training as a chef and food technician. For several years he has been cooking vegan food and following a vegan lifestyle. His internet cooking show and blog with his new vegan creations are a source of constant inspiration.

Daniela Lais was a freelance journalist for many years and she currently works for the vegan bakery at the long-established vegetarian-vegan restaurant Ginko in Graz. Daniela Lais has been vegan for over a decade and she has been involved in vegan baking for more than fifteen years.

... WOULD LIKE TO THANK

Thank you to my wife Melanie (for her patience with me), our kids, our unborn veggie baby and also my parents. Thanks must also go to: Franz and Traute, Marius and Frauke, the Keller family, Dr. Norbert Knitsch, the Eckmeier clan from the Ruhr region, the guys at Budo Nüttermoor, my sensei Hardwig Tomic, Markus at Little Harbour Tattoo, the German Vegetarian Association (VEBU), Bernd Drosihn at tofutown, Sebastian Bete from the OZ, Erwin and Sandra, Ingo Jäger, Tatjana and Boris Seifert, Brigitte "sunshine" Kelly, Nicole Bader, Andreas Kessemeier and the staff at Pool Position, Mike Beuger at the law firm WBS in Cologne, Vik and Tina, the team at VHS Leer, the magazine "Vegetarisch Fit", cinemadirekt Berlin, Keimling Naturkost healthfood store, Jan Bredack and his family, the team at Veganz, Baola in Munich, Chris from myey.info, Roadhouse Herbrum and all you rock 'n' roll guys who have supported me in my work.

Huge thanks to DK, Sarah Fischer, Sabine Durdel-Hoffmann, Jérôme Eckmeier and the German Vegetarian Association (VEBU). To my partner Michael, who always gave my dishes a critical appraisal and who was often required to eat far too much cake. To my parents and all my friends who have backed me up and supported me at every stage, to everyone who is committed to animal rights. Thanks to the Ginko restaurant in Graz, to Esmée and Albin Gilma for the creative freedom they have granted me. I want to thank everyone who has inspired me on my journey, including the many critics; they have helped me become even more motivated and resolved to continue on this path.

We are grateful to the following companies for their kind support: Soyatoo! cream, Viana – smoked tofu, Baola, Keimling Naturkost healthfood store, myey.info, Veganz – we love life, www.alles-vegetarisch.de

Photography Brigitte Sporrer
Food styling Julia Skowronek
Editorial Sabine Durdel-Hoffmann
Design Sonja Gagel
VEBU Coordination Bettina Paul
Title and chapter design Ernesto Kofla

For DK Germany
Publisher Monika Schlitzer
Project manager Sarah Fischer
Production manager Dorothee Whittaker
Production controller Arnika Marx
Producer Inga Reinke

For DK UK
Translator Alison Tunley
Editor Claire Cross
Senior editor Kathryn Meeker
Senior art editor Glenda Fisher
Producer, pre-production Robert Dunn
Producer Stephanie McConnell
Creative technical support Sonia Charbonnier
Managing editor Stephanie Farrow
Managing art editor Christine Keilty

First British Edition, 2018
Dorling Kindersley Limited
One Embassy Gardens, 8 Viaduct Gardens,
London, SW11 7BW
A Penguin Random House company

A CIP catalogue record for this book
is available from the British Library.
ISBN: 978-0-2413-6198-6

Printed and bound in Latvia

A WORLD OF IDEAS:
SEE ALL THERE IS TO KNOW

www.dk.com